# *Why the World Is Full of Useless Things*

## Steve McKevitt

*For Fiona*

© 2006 Steve McKevitt

lished in 2006 by Cyan Books, an imprint of:

Communications Limited
Wardour Street
ndon W1F 0UW
nited Kingdom
Γ: +44 (0)20 7565 6120
E: sales@cyanbooks.com
*www.cyanbooks.com*

The right of Steve McKevitt to be identified as the author of this work has been asserted by him in accordance with the Copyright, Designs and Patents Act 1988.

A CIP record for this book is available from the British Library

ISBN 13  978-1-905736-02-7
ISBN 10  1-905736-02-9

Illustrations by Finger Industries, Sheffield, www.fingerindustries.co.uk

Typeset by Phoenix Photosetting, Lordswood, Chatham, Kent
Printed and bound in Great Britain by
TJ International, Padstow, Cornwall

# Contents

**Part One:**   **Hubris**

**Part Two:**   **Ignorance**

# Acknowledgements

I would like to acknowledge gratefully the assistance of the following people who helped me while I was putting this book together:

Stuart for his continued support and enthusiasm.

Fiona for allowing me the time and space to write and for playing the role of literary editor with aplomb.

Nick, Martin, Dan, Ian and everyone else at the Designers Republic (and in Nick's case special thanks for his extensive knowledge of the moonlighting exploits of former Radio 1 DJs).

Jonny and Marcus at Finger Industries.

Ciaran for bringing to my attention many useless things over the years.

Niamh, Evan and Aoife for being good!

## About the Author

Steve was born in Liverpool, right at the very end of 1966. He began his career in the music industry in the 1980s and has worked all over Europe. He now lives in Sheffield, the UK's finest city, and is happily married with three children.

He has written for many publications including the *Guardian* and the *Independent*.

You can contact him by emailing

steve@mckevittandkenwood.co.uk

If you're not abusive, he might even reply.

# Foreword

I want to start by answering two of the questions that I will inevitably be asked. No, I'm not a grumpy old man and no, I don't hate modern life.

Quite the opposite is true in fact. I'm actually very happy with my life and don't think the world is a wholly bad place; I just think we could do much better. And I don't mean in a deeply spiritual or political way, but in a pragmatic – lots of the stuff we surround ourselves with and consider to be very important is in fact rubbish – kind of a way.

I wrote this book because I was tired of faux nostalgia. I spent most of the 1970s and 1980s hoping that things were going to get better. Despite what B-list celebrities may tell you in *I ♥ the '70s/'80s* et al., they were very dull times. My kids rarely tell me they are bored; I was bored pretty much all the time. Certainly more bored than my parents' generation had been, albeit in their case largely owing to the fact they had been dodging the Luftwaffe's bombs during their formative years. The Second World War was many things, but it was never boring.

What we had when I grew up was optimism; optimism born out of a faith in science and technology and a belief that combining them with good, old-fashioned, British know-how would deliver a better world.

They haven't. They've delivered a different one. One that's full to the brim with crap stuff. Technology remains a part of modern life, but as far as science is concerned, we've never forgiven it.

## One useful thing

*Why the World is Full of Useless Things* was written using OpenOffice.org Writer. OpenOffice is a brilliant suite of open-source software that does everything Microsoft Office does except it's free and – in my opinion – easier to use. Users also experience the bonus of not having that smug paperclip twat turning up every five minutes with his false promises of help.

Microsoft Word is full of apparently useless features. I wonder, for example, whether anyone has ever used the Autosummarize option and, as if by magic, received a word-perfect 300-word precis of their document?

Download it from OpenOffice.org and save yourself several hundred pounds.

Interestingly, in January 2005 Bill Gates allegedly branded all open-source programmers "communists".

The revolution starts here.

*Steve McKevitt*
*SoYo*
*August 2006*

# Preface: The Story of Just One Useless Thing

In April 2003 I was getting ready to leave a very comfortable, well-paid job and strike out on my own. If you've ever tried it yourself, you'll know getting a new business off the ground on your own is quite demanding and you need all the help and support you can get. That is why I shall be forever grateful to a very good friend of mine called Ian, who provided me with short-term office accommodation, telephones, furniture and the loan of a couple of computers for the cost of a pint of beer. In fact, I was so appreciative that while I was buying Ian that pint of beer, I offered to return the favour immediately, inadvertently providing myself with the starting point for this book.

You see, Ian had a product and an opportunity to promote it on television. The only problem was, he didn't have anybody willing to go on TV and promote it for him. With likely candidates thin on the ground, Ian wondered whether or not I knew anyone who, you know, might be willing to do it for him, Steve.

To be fair to Ian, I did have a bit of previous in this area. Some years ago, I earned a living as the PR manager of a video games company – Ian's video games company in fact. In truth this was a rather grand title for a job that often involved little more than showing video games to video games journalists and trying to persuade them to write nice things about them. Of course I said yes. It seemed a small price to pay for a free office, and a speedy way of repaying a mate who'd helped out in my hour of need.

Before we move to the main story, it's probably worth giving you a bit of background about the product itself. At the time Ian was the CEO of an exciting company which was turning heads on the London Stock Exchange with its innovative software targeted at the entertainment industry. His company was in a strong position, cash-rich as a result of successfully taking over a struggling technology business that had no revenue but rather a lot of money in the bank. That struggling company had been called Kazoo and the product Ian wanted me to promote had come as part of the deal.

Kazoo had been a one-product business, and it's difficult to describe its one product, Kazoo 3D, as anything other than a disaster. Kazoo was only one year old when Ian took it over. Things had looked very different twelve months before when Kazoo started trading. It had £12 million in the bank (all raised on the stock market, so technically not even its own money), immediately blew a few million by opening a US office, and invested further millions into product development and marketing: preparing to launch Kazoo 3D on an expectant world.

So what was Kazoo 3D? A cancer cure? A new, greener fuel? A prototype matter-transporter?

No, Kazoo 3D was in fact a software package, available only as an online download,* which allowed you to put 3D models into digital photographs. That's it really. If

---

* Or "Not Available in the Shops", as they used to say about Richard Clayderman albums in the 1980s. If you ever heard one you would know why.

you're still struggling to get your head around the concept, remember those Photo-Me booths where you could choose to have your picture taken so it would look as if you were with Jet from *Gladiators* or Take That? Well, like that, only with a cartoon character – like Mickey Mouse or Scooby Doo – dropped into the photograph by you, at home, without any need for a Photo-Me booth ... except they couldn't afford to license Scooby Doo and, as Disney are pretty keen to control what you can and can't do with an image of Mickey Mouse, they had to use cartoon characters you've never heard of – like one of a cat in a bow tie, or a fox carrying a tray, or a dog with a guitar.

Customers could pay to download additional themed model packs – the self-explanatory Christmas or Dinosaurs, for example – and use them to make cards, calendars ... um, anything, really. It couldn't fail.

At the end of its first year of trading, Kazoo published its accounts. Having spent the best part of £6 million developing Kazoo 3D and taking it to market, the company had sold almost £1,000 worth of stock. I'll do the maths for you: that's a loss of £6 million, or £500,000 a month or £125,000 each week. Whatever way you look at it, it's a lot of money to lose.

At this point, Ian took over Kazoo and set its technical team to work on developing something altogether more saleable. But, ever the entrepreneur, Ian couldn't help wondering whether there wasn't something worth salvaging from the wreckage of Kazoo 3D; after all, over £6 million had been spent developing it – and that should surely count for something, shouldn't it?

Despite its spectacular failure, there is no denying that Kazoo 3D was a very clever product. Underlying its simple interface was some powerful rendering technology. Rendering is a process of creating computer images from models, the kind used by architects to show what their designs will look like as finished buildings. Anyone with a technical background couldn't help but marvel at the quality of Kazoo's light-sourcing and the speed at which it rendered finished pictures. No, the technology was absolutely sound – it was just that no one could work out what you were supposed to do with it (beyond cards, calendars, anything ...).

Undeterred, Ian decided to take a punt. Focus-grouping the product within an inch of its life, his marketing team decided that it was: "A fun product: one that allowed a rare opportunity for parents and children to spend quality creative time together, at the computer, having fun with 3D models and digital photographs."

They spent a few thousand quid putting some decent packaging together and changed the name to the more prosaic, but arguably more customer-friendly, Home Creative Studio, with a view to selling it in shops.

His first setback came when the world of retail proved unwilling to stock Home Creative Studio. The problem remained that, yes, the technology was very clever, but beyond "cards, calendars, anything ...", what could you actually do with it? And in any case, where would it go in the shop? Was it a game or a professional artwork package?

Retailers don't have elastic shelves, nor are they short of

people wanting to give them stuff to sell on them. The stock retailer response to any new product is, "I don't want any and I want it for less."

Never one to give up easily, Ian tried again with mail-order catalogues, and when that didn't work, again with a different online approach. All this effort was to no avail; no matter what he did, it seemed, Home Creative Studio just wouldn't sell. Yet still Ian didn't lose faith in the product. His daughter and her friends loved playing with it, making cards, calendars, anything – if only he could just get people to see how much fun Home Creative Studio was, he was sure it would fly out.

It was now that serendipity offered him just such an opportunity. Barry, the company sales director, had pulled in a few favours and secured Ian a slot on QVC, the world's biggest home-shopping TV channel.

For those of you unfamiliar with it, QVC is an alternative reality, discovered by Joseph Segel (I think he was a physicist) in 1986. Through a break in the space–time continuum, QVC beams television pictures down to us on Planet Earth, reaching over 144 million televisions across the world.

The alternative QVC reality is very similar to our own, with just a few curious colloquialisms – glass beads are called Diamonique, for example. In fact, the only fundamental difference, as far as I can tell, is that life on QVC is much, much more boring than it is here on earth. As a result people in QVC get very excited about things that we on earth would consider to be deeply uninteresting and mundane, even humble household objects like squeegees, bottle openers, penknives or duvet covers can drive them to fits of apoplexy.

Is any of this true? I dunno, but I find this explanation less amazing that the official version, which is that QVC employs 1,800 people and reaches 15.6 million households every week in the United Kingdom alone. Last year it sold £265 million worth of goods, shipping 10.2 million packages and taking 13.2 million phone calls.

Barry assured Ian that he'd be amazed at how much product QVC shifted.

"How much?" asked Ian

"Shitloads!" replied Barry.

Ian was amazed. All he needed to do was to find somebody willing to go on TV and demonstrate it for him. This is where I came in.

Anyway, back to the story. It quickly transpired that my appearance on QVC was not a given. The world's number-one home-shopping channel is apparently quite picky about who it will allow to appear on-screen. They won't have any old Tom, Dick or, in this instance, Steve. So it was that I was dispatched a few weeks later to undergo my first ever – and to date only – TV audition; one that would determine whether my presentation skills passed muster.

I arrived at QVC's Battersea studio (a building formerly occupied by the *Observer* and the less enduring On-Digital) and was met by a friendly producer called Jess. Jess explained to me that the thing to remember was, when all was said and done, that QVC was a television show. That meant it was as much about entertainment as it was about selling things. I swallowed this information as easily as a pint of paracetamol. Jess went on to explain that, should my audition go to plan, I would be appearing the following week on *QVC Selection*. She described *QVC Selection*, broadcast every Sunday at 3 p.m., as "a programme featuring some of the most popular items selected from across QVC's product range. It's a veritable potpourri of bargains specially recommended by the channel". I felt a more appropriate title might have been *Stuff that Doesn't Really Fit in Anywhere Else*. Like, say, Home Creative Studio.

*QVC Selection* is presented by Kathy Tayler. Kathy is a former British gymnast whom you may dimly recall from a twelve-year stint on the BBC *Holiday Programme*; think Lorraine Kelly without the urban edginess.

We were introduced and went through to the studio. Kathy was easy – politeness itself:

"Hi, Steve, I hear you've got something really exciting for us today."

Wow, she seemed genuinely interested.

"Yes, Kathy, I have, it's called Home Creative Studio and it's a great fun product, which allows you to have fun with 3D models and digital photographs. It provides a rare opportunity for parents and children to spend quality time at the computer, having fun with 3D models and digital photographs. On your computer. It's great fun."

"Really?"

"Yes, Kathy. The underlying technology in Home Creative Studio is really powerful – it's used by architects and engineers – and it allows you to manipulate fantastic 3D models and drop them into your digital photos. It's great fun. And you can use the finished pictures to make cards, calendars, anything … It's great fun."

Jess cut me off. My audition was over almost as soon as it had started. You'll be delighted to hear I hadn't lost any of the old magic and had come through with flying colours. Jess confirmed the details of my live appearance, which would take place on the library set.

How long, I wondered, would I be on for?

Jess smiled. "If it goes well, you could be on for the whole hour."

Crikey! A whole hour talking about Home Creative Studio! I've been to lectures on the Thirty Years War that didn't last that long. She must have read my mind.

"Don't worry about it, Kathy will guide you through it. You just have to go over the same points again and again. It's easy, I'm sure you'll be fine. Oh, and dress smart-casual."

I relaxed. Jess was right; of course I would be fine – I had Kathy there to guide me. I would be dressed in relaxing smart-casual. Everything was going brilliantly. Ian had every reason to be pleased.

We decided to make a weekend of Home Creative Studio's TV debut and stayed with some friends, Ciaran and Suzanne, in North London. Ciaran was a PR specialising in the video games and leisure software business, so he expressed a polite and professional interest in the object of my visit. He was in the middle of clearing out his home office; consequently his dining-room table was piled two feet high with what looked like a lifetime's supply of boxed computer games and leisure software. He'd seen a lot of this kind of thing.

I loaded up Home Creative Studio for him, interested to see what an expert made of it. I spun a model of a pink cat in a bow tie and dropped it into a picture featuring Ciaran's two kids on a family holiday. He was immediately impressed.

"That's very clever. The underlying technology must be really powerful. People won't realise how difficult it is to pull that sort of thing off. It must have cost a fortune to develop."

Told you he was technical.

"About six million quid," I replied.

"Wow! Now that is a fortune. Or at least, it was some-body's fortune." He took the mouse from me and started playing about with it. "What's it for?"

"It's about having fun with digital photography." I was into my patter. "It offers a rare opportunity for parents and kids to spend quality time at the computer, having fun with 3D models and digital photographs."

Ciaran started to laugh, "Right. OK ... But what is it *actually* for?"

"You can use it to make calendars, cards, anything."

Ciaran was rotating a model of a velociraptor so that it looked as if it was biting his wife's head off. "Hmm, how long are you on for?"

"They said I could be on for an hour."

"Well, that's going to be appointment viewing, isn't it? Let's just hope you've got enough 'anything' examples to keep you going. Either that or you're going to be making one hell of a birthday card."

I started perusing the mountain of leisure software.

"It's like an Aladdin's cave of shite, isn't it?" I remarked, idly inspecting the blurb on the back of *The Interactive Oasis Songbook*. "You look at all this and you realise, the world really is full of product."

I started sifting through the boxes. I was drawn to one in psychedelic packaging that was snappily titled *Haight-Ashbury in the Sixties*. I had no idea who Haight Ashbury was. It turned out to be not a "he", but an "it". The CD-ROM promised to re-create the spirit of the Haight-Ashbury culture of San Francisco in the late sixties. I read on with interest.

"*Tune In* focuses on the *San Francisco Oracle* and the art and articles that appeared in it. *Turn On* allows players to experience the art and music of the '60s. *Drop Out* is a game for up to six people where the focus is to be the first to experience enlightenment by gathering the requisite number of food and shelter, spirituality, hipness and love points."

I was unsurprised to see this was still shrink-wrapped.

"Who do you think bought this?" said Ciaran, holding up *The Secrets of Stargate*. He read aloud from the back: "'A multimedia behind-the-scenes look at the hit movie.' Can't wait!"

Unfortunately, given that I don't think too many people had been motivated to look at the film itself, let alone behind the scenes, I think *The Secrets of Stargate* are likely to remain so in perpetuity. This is a pity really, because if more people had seen the film, then more people would have realised what a shocking waste of creative effort it was.

"Look at this," Ciaran said, handing me a copy of *The Interactive Bible (with commentary by Charlton Heston)*. "How's that for ambition? Nothing less than an attempt to actually improve on the Word of God. Now that's a product designer with confidence."

Sunday was the hottest day of the year so far. Ciaran's car was lacking air con, so even with the windows open, travelling at central London speed meant that I was sweating like a drugs mule in the "nothing to declare" channel by the time we pulled up at QVC. The skeleton weekend staff lent the huge building a ghostly quality. It was virtually deserted. I was eventually met in reception by a very flustered Jess, who ushered me up three flights of stairs to the green room.

"We're dreadfully short-staffed today," she explained. "We've got two people off sick." She eyed the beads of perspiration rolling down my forehead. "I think it's the heat."

Eventually we arrived, and Jess told me to help myself to tea or coffee and that she would be back shortly to take me on to the set.

The green room was rather disappointing: more like a dentist's waiting room that a celebrity bolt-hole. At least the chairs looked comfy, and along with the piles of dog-eared editions of *Take a Break* and *Heat* there were two large TV monitors on the wall to keep us entertained. One of these was, naturally, showing QVC, the other appeared to be some kind of live Excel spreadsheet and, as such, was obviously far more interesting.

I had a raging thirst and so I helped myself to a refreshing cup of stale coffee. There were two other people in the green room, whom I correctly identified as fellow guests. Sitting on one of the comfy chairs was a pensive-looking man in his mid-fifties. Despite the heat, he was dressed in a cardigan with leather patches on the sleeves. He looked as if he'd being doing the garden. He was toying rather disconcertingly with what looked like the world's smallest flick-knife. The other person was an American woman of indeterminate age. You could tell instantly she was American – it was a look you never see on anyone else. The hairstyle said 20, the face said 60, the CV probably said 49, but the outfit simply screamed, "I'm very rich and, as you can see, money can't buy taste." Imagine the Queen Mum turning up at a fancy dress party as one of the Bratz dolls and you're almost there.

A harsh assessment perhaps, from an overweight thirtysomething, who looked like he'd run the London Marathon fully clothed, but fair none the less. She was staring intently at the Live Excel spreadsheet. I picked up an issue of *Take a Break* and read an article on batik.

Jess popped her head round the door, and asked whether Geoff and his short-blade pocket chainsaw ("Ah, that's what it is!") would like to follow her to the garden set. The nervous man rose to his feet ponderously and obediently shuffled after Jess.

I finished the article on batik and toyed with the idea of doing a word search in my head before remembering that they are not that much fun, even when you've got a pen.

I looked up at the monitor to see that Geoff was now live on-screen. He was just starting his presentation of the short-blade pocket chainsaw. Strangely, he didn't look nervous any more, he looked very excited – reminiscent of a speed addict, in fact – and he was talking about his short-blade pocket chainsaw with all the passion and sincerity of a born-again Christian. He was certainly converting me. I started to wonder how I'd ever lived without a short-blade pocket chainsaw. Four minutes into his presentation, he cut through a solid steel rod two inches thick. If I'd had a remote control to hand I would have been pressing "Buy".

"Ha! They'll get him to show that again."

It was the American Bratz OAP. She was still staring intently at the screen, but as there was no one else around I guessed that she was talking to me.

"What do you mean?"

She made no eye contact, transfixed by the screen. She pointed to one of the columns on the spreadsheet thing.

"See here? Well, that's a list of all the products they are going to be selling today. And in that column next to it? You see that moving number? Well, that's the number of people who've ordered his product. After he cut through that steel rod, there was a big spike in the number of orders."

Sure enough, there on-screen was a list of maybe twenty items. The number next to the short-blade chainsaw (listed, I noted, just above Home Creative Studio) was rapidly clocking up. In just five minutes Geoff had sold almost 1,800 units. Barry was right on both counts. I was amazed at how much you could sell on QVC.

And it was shitloads.

"Crikey, I didn't realise there were that many people watching."

"Oh, this is very a quiet time," my Bratz buddy explained. "They test out things here to see how well they sell, but you can do much more in the evenings. I've sold thirty thousand units no problem before now, but I've gotta new range of jewellery out and they thought they'd test it now before going to peak time."

Geoff's performance was still electric, but I noticed his numbers were going up much more slowly now. Still, he had sold well over 2,500 chainsaws in less than ten minutes. Clearly I had much to learn. Fortunately I also had a willing teacher.

"Ha! They'll definitely be asking him back. Those kind of gadgets do really well. And £13.72 is a great price point."

"It is," I concurred. "You sound like you know your stuff. Do you come here often?"

I became suddenly conscious that it sounded as if I was chatting her up. She made eye contact for the first time.

"Twice a month, every month. I pretty much clear thirty thousand dollars' profit every time. How about you?"

"I've never done this kind of thing before. It's my first time."

"What are you showing?"

"Home Creative Studio. It's a great fun product that allows you to have fun with 3D models and digital photographs."

"Best of luck."

Thankfully, the unintentional sexual tension I was building up was relieved by the return of Jess. Geoff's numbers were slowing down, she explained, so would I like to follow her to the library.

Most people will tell you TV studios are surprisingly small. Unless, that is, they've been on QVC. It was huge. Jess led me quietly to a set that was a fairly good facsimile of a library. Bookcases lined the walls and in front of them a pair of winged armchairs straddled a walnut bureau, on which sat a PC with Home Creative Studio already running.

The illusion was broken only by the fact that where the library's fourth wall should have been was the brightly lit garden set, in which Geoff was sawing through a two-inch steel bar for the fourth time.

Kathy arrived and smiled a welcome. "Hello again, Steve. It's a lovely day, isn't it? I'd much rather be outdoors than in here. No offence."

"None taken," I replied.

"Ready to go," said Jess, "in five, four ..."

And finally we were off.

> *Kathy Tayler*: Hello and welcome to this week's edition of *QVC Selection*, where we'll be featuring some of the most popular items selected from across QVC's product range as well as some exciting first-time-on-QVC bargains. We've got some fabulous jewellery coming up a bit later on, but before then we've got something very exciting for you. It's a fun computer product called Home Creative Studio, and Steve

McKevitt has come all the way from Sheffield to show it to us. Hello, Steve.

*Steve McKevitt*: Hello, Kathy.

(How exciting, not an autocue in sight – we were making it up as we went along.)

*Kathy Tayler*: So, Steve, what exactly is Home Creative Studio?

*Steve McKevitt*: Well, Kathy, that's a very good question. As you can see HCS, as we call it, is a great fun product that allows you to have fun with 3D models and digital photos. And that provides a rare opportunity for parents and children to spend quality creative time together, at the computer, having fun with digital photographs. And 3D models.

(Remember, Steve, don't show the product: sell the product!)

*Kathy Tayler*: Because if you're like me, you take all these digital photos and you never know what to do with them.

*Steve McKevitt*: That's exactly right!

(Jeez, Kathy's good! I'd never thought of that one before. I wonder whether we had a sales spike there?)

*Kathy Tayler*: So how does it work?

> *Steve McKevitt*: HCS is a very clever
> product. Underlying it is some powerful
> technology, like the kind used by architects
> to show what their designs will look like as
> finished buildings. It allows you to put
> amazing 3D models into digital photographs
> to make cards, calendars ... um, anything,
> really. Let me show you ...

And boy, did I show them what a fun product it was. I had fun putting a 3D model of a teddy bear with a sombrero into a digital photo of a kid's birthday party and made a fantastic greetings card. I had fun putting a 3D model of a vintage car and another of a hot-air balloon into a snow scene and made a fun calendar. And, in a moment of inspiration, I even had fun dropping a 3D model of a Tyrannosaurus rex into a picture of myself, and created a side-splitting visual gag by making it look as if the monster was biting my head off! Kathy was lapping it up.

I was just putting the finishing touches to a fun Christmas card featuring 3D models of Humpty Dumpty and a giant plum duff when Kathy smiled, thanked me and moved efficiently on to the next item.

It was not a moment too soon. I really did have nothing left to say about fun, 3D models, kids, cards, calendars or anything. We'd been on air for twenty minutes, but it felt like four times that long.

Jess appeared, like the shopkeeper from *Mr Benn*, and ushered me from the set.

"You did really, really well. Fantastic. That game thing looks great; you must send me down a copy."

"No problem at all, Jess. How did it sell?"

"Well, we won't really know until tomorrow. The orders will come in throughout the rest of the day."

"Ballpark figure?"

Jess was getting cagey.

"Sorry, I wouldn't like to say. It's against company policy."

"I understand. Oh, by the way, I think I left my bag in the green room. Can I just nip back and get it?"

"I'll get if for you, if you want to wait here."

"No, Jess, it's no problem, you don't know what it looks like."

I darted left into the green room before she could object. It was empty now. I made straight for the Excel spreadsheet. It read:

| | | | |
|---|---|---|---|
| 14.20 | till-a-matic.soil.culti | £94.92 | 000894 |
| 14.40 | short-blade.pkt.ch-sw | £13.72 | 003103 |
| 15.00 | home.creative.studio | £39.95 | 000026 |

"Don't worry. It could easily be double that number by tomorrow morning." If Jess was trying to help she had a failed miserably. We walked to reception in silence.

"Well, here we are," said Jess nervously. "See you again."

I smiled. "I doubt it."

Twenty-six! Twenty fucking six! In terms of development money that's £230,769.23 each. I never did find out if it doubled overnight.

That was the last time I ever saw Home Creative Studio, Jess, QVC or Kathy Tayler. I think even Ian admitted defeat after that. We'd barely recouped the cost of my train fare.

Twenty-six!

One thing that has fascinated me ever since is how did we come to waste so much time and energy on such an obvious turkey? Ian's no fool, and Home Creative Studio is not an aberration. This is the story of how the world became full of useless things and how we came to be spending so much of our time so uselessly. Read on, if you dare.

I ask you, though – 26!

Part One | **Hubris**

**Hubris:** *noun:* excessive pride or self-confidence. *Origin* Greek, originally denoting presumption towards or defiance of the gods, leading to nemesis. The false belief that one is a god or that one has god-like powers.

# 1 | **Tomorrow's World**

"We have never had it so good."
*Harold Macmillan, former*
*Conservative prime minister*

We are constantly reminded there has never been a better time than now to be a consumer. The argument goes like this. We earn far more on average than any of our ancestors up to and including our parents, and if you've got the necessary disposable income, you can pretty much buy whatever you want from the comfort of your living room. In fact, you don't even need the disposable income. We also have the ability to borrow what these same ancestors would consider untold riches. Simply make a quick call to a bank, credit card or loan company, and you're just minutes away from being able to pretend you've got the necessary disposable income. This is in fact what most of us do.

And it is exactly because we have more money to spend than ever before that, surprise, surprise, there are more things to spend it on than ever before.

So there you have it – we consumers are literally spoilt for choice: our world is full of all the product, entertainment and amenity we could ever want.

Now there is a downside, of course. Most of the products you can buy are, as Gerald Ratner once said, complete crap. Gerry might have been demonised at the time for telling the truth, but twelve years on, his ill-advised comments appear less prophetic but more like a starting gun for the Ratnerisation of every area of society.

Reviews sections and magazines have expanded to cope with consumer demand for buying advice. There's a guilty pleasure to be had reading damning reviews – they are invariably more entertaining than glowing eulogies – but every day, thousands of useless products are being foisted upon target markets that never knew they wanted them. Billions of pounds will be wasted in vain attempts to convince the target market that their time-poor lives will be improved if they'd only agree to make themselves less cash-rich and purchase this particular piece of tat.

Most of the things produced by most of the companies in the world are destined to fail: 85 per cent of new products launched fail in the first year. What's more, right the way through the development cycle everybody involved with bringing the product to market, from lab technicians and programmers through to marketers and sales people, knew that the product was destined to fail.

In the UK, 75 per cent of start-up businesses go to the wall before they are twelve months old. Of those that survive, 75 per cent will have gone to the wall before they are three years old.* In fact, they were destined to fail from the second they were conceived. Businesses fail for many reasons, but it's fair to say that many of them do because not enough people want the products or services they are trying to sell.

I often think how disappointed ten-year-old me would be if he could visit me today, in what would be, to him, 30 years in the future.

---

* Source: Business Link, 2004.

I was ten years old in 1976. I was a pretty unremark-
able kid, interested in most of the things ten-year-olds are
supposed to be interested in. Some of these interests have
stayed with me. I was already obsessed with football and
there were early signs that my other great passion – for
music – was starting to develop. I was too young to
understand, or even notice, the cultural revolution that
was being led by the Sex Pistols, but I was already a
proud owner of a copy of ABBA's greatest-hits album. I
had also started to have confused, but ultimately pure,
feelings for Louise Pope, the very pretty girl who sat at
my table and shared my passion for colouring things in.

Life was relatively uncomplicated. True, I was appre-
hensive about moving up to comprehensive school, but I
firmly believed that the fact I'd recently been awarded a
Silver Arrow badge at Cubs would stand me in good
stead. According to my diary, my literary interests were
largely restricted to *Roy of the Rovers* and *Asterix the
Gaul*, and my top-five favourite TV programmes were
*Match of the Day, Star Trek, The Goodies, Doctor
Who* and perhaps a less obvious choice, *Tomorrow's
World*.

The public attitude towards science in the mid-1970s
was far more positive than it is today. The moon landings
were still fresh in the memory and science was promising
that its discoveries would yield a bright new tomorrow of
space travel, increased leisure time and the opportunity to
marry a clone of Raquel Welch. I shared the prevailing
wisdom that science was a panacea for the world's ills and,
as far as I was concerned, *Tomorrow's World* offered a

sneaky-peek preview of how I could expect to be living my adult life.

Scheduled at 7 p.m. on Thursday evenings – in between *Nationwide* and *Top of the Pops* – *Tomorrow's World* was presented by ex-Spitfire pilot Raymond Baxter. Born in the white heat of Harold Wilson's technological revolution, *TW*'s format was simple. Each week, a selection of gee-whizz inventions and amazing scientific breakthroughs were presented in turn. Baxter was ably assisted by a team that included blond no-nonsense action man William Woollard (who may or may not have once dated Princess Anne), and the painfully articulate Judith Hann. Hann presented her items in the manner of a rather game supply teacher working with an unfamiliar subject. The only thing the items had in common was their potential to change the world we live in.

Each item lasted about five minutes and invariably followed the same formula. One of life's problems would be presented – anything from opening a bottle of wine if you were left-handed to building a city on Mars – followed by a description of the invention that provided the solution. Items ended with a short practical demonstration of variable quality and success, and for which we would be asked to keep our fingers crossed. The money shot was provided by a prediction about when we could expect that the said innovation would achieve widespread acceptance, based on the opinions of a mysterious group of unseen "experts".

Every week, I'd sit enthralled by this window that had been thrown open on the future. I'd calculate how old I'd be when I'd own the robotic grabber developed by students at St Andrews University, or be sitting down to a plate of Christmas-dinner-flavoured salad – possibly with Louise and our kids.

My entertainment was only mildly spoiled by the cynicism of my father, who would look up periodically from the sports pages of the *Daily Mirror* to scoff loudly at the experts' predictions.

"If I had an invention, the last people I'd tell about it are that bloody shower," would open a typical put-down. "It's the kiss of death going on this show – you never hear of any of these things again."

*Tomorrow's World* ran for almost thirty years. I bet if my Luddite dad had seen the episode where Judith Hann smeared jam on a compact disc, scratched it with a knife and still managed to get it to work, he'd be eating those words today!

As ten-year-old me would attest during his visit to 2006, *Tomorrow's World* got it wrong, but in that sense it is no different to any other attempt to predict the future. Given that predicting the future is – well, let's face it – fundamentally impossible, it's surprising for just how many professions it's a basic requirement. From economists, stockbrokers and weathermen to astrologers, professional gamblers and advertising execs, much of the job involves attempting to state, in a manner that sounds as if there's at least a degree of certainty, what will happen next.

The good news is, because it's impossible to predict the future, no one will blame you if you get it wrong. In fact, you only have to get it right once in a while (witness Judith Hann and her strawberry-preserve CD) and in that respect at least you'll have the law of averages on your side. Believe me, there are harder jobs.

Once he got over the delight of seeing that I'd made it through big school alive, ten-year-old me would struggle to hide his disappointment at the fact that I'd failed to make the grade as either a professional footballer or – his fall-back career – an astronaut. Although it will pain my lovely wife to hear me say this, I know he'd be devastated to see that the colouring in hadn't been enough to hold us together and that the woman I'd chosen to settle down with wasn't Louise Pope. But these would just be minor personal let-downs compared to his wider devastation at how little we'd appeared to have moved forward since 1976.

If my mother's to be believed, one thing's for sure: ten-year-old me would start asking a hell of a lot of questions. And I've no doubt which one would be top of the list: why the hell are you still driving around in a car and why are kids still going to school on the bus?

The thing is, I'd know exactly what he means and the specific event he's referring to. Let's return briefly to 1976 while I explain.

For ten-year-old me in 1976, being ill was not necessarily a bad thing, especially if I was lucky enough to be caught in the hinterland of not actually feeling that terrible, but remaining too infectious to go to school.

It was on one such day during the autumn term that I found myself proclaimed too ill to attend St Johns RC Junior School. Stifling my euphoria, I just about managed to walk – in what I imagined was a very ill and enfeebled

manner – downstairs to the sofa, where Mum had prepared a sickbed with cushions and blankets. I waved my
younger brother off to school, heartened by the knowledge
that boiled egg and soldiers would be arriving any minute
now, and that, strengthened by this repast, I would now be
spending the rest of the day in front of the TV.

For those of you too young to remember, it's worth
pointing out that daytime TV in 1976 was a very different
proposition to the daytime TV we know today.

For a start, the concept of daytime TV didn't exist. TV
executives clearly didn't believe anyone would want to
watch TV during the day: we were all too busy working,
going to school or doing the housework (I've no idea what
undergraduates did during the day back then).

BBC1 had just made friends with the fact that people
might have a bit of time on their hands over lunch, and
reluctantly gave us a couple of hours of programming.
Things kicked off with a quick news bulletin normally read
by Kenneth Kendal, followed by *Pebble Mill at One*,*
*Andy Pandy* or a similar tots programme in the *Watch
with Mother* slot. Things culminated at about 2.25 with an
episode of the – some would way – insensitively scheduled

---

* *Pebble Mill* ... was a magazine show broadcast live from Birmingham in
front of an audience whose average age was 160. A kind of proto *Richard
and Judy* with the sexual frisson removed, it was anchored by Donny
MacLeod and Bob Langley. A typical show would kick off with a recipe
for lamb casserole, a fashion item about rising/falling hemlines, an interview with Olympic shotputter Geoff Capes doing something requiring
great strength, then over to Peter Seabrook in the greenhouse before things
were rounded off with by a musical performance of "What Did
Delaware?" by Kenny Ball's Jazzmen.

Welsh-language programme *Lechyd Da*. Presumably this was either peak viewing time in Bangor, or Anne Robinson started her career in scheduling.

With *Pebble Mill* ... still a good four hours away, my sickbed entertainment would be provided by nothing less than *ITV for Schools and Colleges*.

ITV began broadcasting schools programmes in 1957. The idea was that television could be as valid a teaching medium as any other; it also gave broadcasters an opportunity to test their signals at a time when it was felt that normal programming could not be supported by advertising. How effective the project was is a moot point, because there were never any studies carried out to see whether children benefited from cabbaging in front of the TV rather than interacting with a teacher. I can't think why this might have been.

In 1976 we took what we could get in terms of TV entertainment, and for a sick boy, with a day on the sofa ahead of him, *ITV for Schools and Colleges* was as good as it got. The programme that had such a profound impact on me that morning was called *Picture Box*. Aimed at eight-to-ten-year-olds and presented by the anodyne Alan Rothwell, it was an apparently random series of films from around the world glued together by the concept "thought provoking". As a result, *Picture Box* was an exercise in pot luck. If you were unlucky this could be a dull study of a tropical reef with nothing more than a xylophone to provide the sonics, but if you were lucky it might be a film about Mars or volcanoes. That day I hit pay dirt: a documentary about the history of jet packs.

It was like the best episode of *Tomorrow's World* ever, I was treated to fifteen minutes of the finest eye candy ever. There were films of men taking off, soaring away over tree-tops "at speeds of up to sixty miles an hour" and then landing in a field and breaking into a little jog. Obviously I'd seen jet packs on TV before – *Diamonds Are Forever* is one of the first films I remember seeing, and that had a jet pack *and* a moon buggy in it* – but this was different: these were real. The Rolls-Royce of jet packs was something the US military was testing called the WASP. In tribute to William Woollard, the voice-over signed off by telling us that "experts" anticipated that the WASP II from Bell Aerosystems (which was mildly less sexy in that you stood in it rather than wore it) would be commercially available within five years.

Thank God Dad wasn't watching with me to pour his foolish scorn on this prediction. I was smart enough to know they wouldn't lie to us in an educational programme, and I calculated that, even allowing for the fact that Dad was not what you'd call an early adopter, this meant that I could reasonably expect to own a jet pack by 1982.

The film finished and cut back to a beaming Rothwell back in the studio: "Would you like to fly around in a jet pack?" he asked, a little superfluously.

"Oh, would I!"

He then added the inevitable educational pay-off: "Perhaps you can imagine what it would be like to fly a jet pack and then write a story about it."

---

* Actually, it might have been *Thunderball*. Who says James Bond films are all the same?

Well, I was officially too ill to write a story, but I took him at his word and spent the rest of the day imagining what it would be like to fly.

I imagined life in the distant future of 1982. I'd be fifteen – me and Louise Pope would probably be going steady by then.

If I wanted to go somewhere I'd just fly, simple as that. The UK's island status would no longer be enough to contain me. I'd soar over forests and mountains, swooping down across the ocean, trailing an arm in the water as the setting sunlight bathed me in a golden glow.

Then I realised that I wouldn't be the only one with a jet pack – all my mates would have one as well. We could fly around in formation having adventures.

Even going to the shops for my mum would become a pleasure rather than a chore. Actually, the WASP II had seemed a little short of luggage space, and I suspected that dangling my shopping from the handlebars might prove a little impractical – it would interfere with the exhaust system. Still, five years to the commercial launch was plenty for the experts to crack any storage issues.

Jet packs were the single most exciting thing I'd ever seen. Come to think of it – given the impact they were going to have on the way we live – it was a little surprising that the manufacturers had decided to launch them on *Picture Box* and not something more auspicious like the *Daily Mirror* or *Granada Reports*. I reminded myself to check the paper when Dad got home. When I did there was, surprisingly, nothing at all about jet packs. Even *Picture Box* didn't get a name check. The TV guide simply said: "9.20–11.55 *ITV for Schools and Colleges*".

I asked Dad whether he thought we'd all be flying round in jet packs in 1982.

He laughed. "Of course we will!" he said, ruffling my hair, before adding, "He's not feeling any better, is he, Mum?" Mum laughed as well.

Things took a further turn for the worse the next day when I told my school friends to forget about their bikes and get ready for the jet pack. They didn't believe me. I was accused of making the whole thing up, just as I had the previous year with my uncle's yellow submarine and the trip to Africa we were all going to make in it. I wasn't as bothered as I might have been. I knew that they'd be laughing on the other side of their faces in a few years' time – jet packs would be all over the TV and I'd be hailed as the Boy Who Had Predicted the Future.

Unfortunately – the Los Angeles Olympics opening ceremony notwithstanding – that was pretty much the last time I ever saw a jet pack.*

In many respects this story sums up the 1970s. A dismal decade of strike and shortage may have shattered the 1960s dream, and just when no one believed things could get any worse, the 1980s happened. Yet despite this, people's optimism for the future was arguably at an all-time high. It was an optimism largely based on scientific

---

* I did see the jet packs on TV once more. Five years later, Kieran Prenderville presented a *Tomorrow's World* item about the WASP II, but this time I was old enough to realise that an appearance on TV really did represent the final nail in the coffin.

innovation and technological breakthroughs which is in stark contrast to opinion today. People take a dim view of science: they have become suspicious of things like GM foods, pharmaceuticals, embryo research, nuclear energy, cloning and computers. Few people believe we will be colonising Mars, living in cities under the sea, marrying Raquel Welch clones or flying around in jet packs any time soon.

In 1976, nobody had a computer, CD player or video recorder, and the most exciting innovation in TV was that new sets were being equipped with a tantalising ITV2 button.* People were, however, getting so used to seeing men walk on the moon that only a near-death experience was enough to get us to tune in to an Apollo mission. Concorde, the fastest passenger plane in the world, had taken air travel supersonic; experts were predicting that computers would soon be doing most of our work for us and for manual work like building cars, we would have robots. Offices in the future would be paperless, factories pitch dark. This was the age of the train. British Rail announced a new high-speed passenger train, and while the Americans were wasting their time with jet packs the Europeans had got together to build the Eurofighter, which would be in service by the early 1980s.

Food shortages would become a thing of the past thanks to a miracle new protein made from soya beans that looked and tasted *exactly* the same as real meat. Slaving

---

* The launch of Channel 4 does little to detract from this commendable "belt and braces" approach in my opinion.

away over the stove would be history. Meals would be sold freeze-dried; they could be rehydrated and heated in a new microwave oven in a matter of minutes.

The only thing people had to worry about was what they were going to do with all their new-found leisure time.

In short this was a time of big scientific leaps forward and people expected these big scientific leaps to continue.

And that is why, when ten-year-old me visits 2006, he's terribly disappointed by what he perceives to be shuffling baby-steps.

Science, it would appear, has stopped trying to answer the big questions and has concentrated on incrementally improving the very small ones. Most of the major life-changing breakthroughs of the last 30 years have been in the fields of telecommunications and computing. Microsoft is the biggest company in the world, not Bell Aerosystems.

We have mobile phones, the Internet, video games consoles, computers and flat-screen TVs, but travel by road is slower than it was 30 years ago and we don't even have Concorde or high-speed trains, let alone space travel. The process of innovation is slowing down. And those speculating what life will be like 30 years into the future do so much less optimistically but, I'm certain, just as inaccurately as ten-year-old me.

## 2 | **Confidently Predicted**

"There are known knowns. These are things
we know that we know. There are known
unknowns. That is to say, there are things that
we know we don't know. But there are also
unknown unknowns. There are things we
don't know we don't know."

*Donald Rumsfeld,*
*21st US Secretary of Defense*

Speculation has always been rife. Whether it's about the
existence of God, the victor in next Saturday's important
league fixture or simply what's for tea, we like nothing
better than wondering what the future will be like. Possibilities, outcomes, likelihoods – this is the stuff of living, as
if all the big issues of Life, the Universe and Everything can
be distilled into one of the more popular rounds on *A
Question of Sport*: what happens next?

I'm not the only person to notice an absence of weekend
breaks on Mars and general flying about. There is a group
of future gazers – including, perhaps inevitably, the odd
"eminent scientist" – that has taken this lack of meaningful
innovation theme and not so much run as sprinted away as
fast as they could with it. That is to say they are boldly predicting the imminent arrival of a second Dark Age.

In October 2005, the *Sunday Times* decided to put this
movement in the spotlight and ran a series of articles drawing on a variety of books and experts (them again). It was
called "Waiting for the Lights to Go Out", and the lead

feature was written by author Bryan Appleyard. In these articles, the usual mix of gloom about climate change and depletion of oil was given a novel twist. It claimed that innovation, the economic driving force of the past 200 years, had slowed to such a dramatic extent that it would severely impede our ability to think of a solution: "Oil is running out; the climate is changing at a potentially catastrophic rate; wars over scarce resources are brewing; finally, most shocking of all, we don't seem to be having enough ideas about how to fix any of these things."

Now, I'm no scientist so I find it very difficult to comment on this, but then neither is Bryan Appleyard. Obviously aware of this fact himself, Appleyard called on the expertise of a US physicist called Jonathan Huebner to provide expert support for his argument. Since 1985, Huebner has worked at the Pentagon's Naval Air Warfare Center in China Lake, California. When he took the job, he expected to witness a huge number of scientific advances, but by 1990 was disappointed by how few he'd seen. He decided to find out why. Appleyard tells us what he found:

> After some elaborate mathematics, he [Huebner] came to a conclusion that raised serious questions about our continued ability to sustain progress. What he found was that the rate of innovation peaked in 1873 and has been declining ever since. In fact, our current rate of innovation – which Huebner puts at seven important technological developments per billion people per year – is about the same

> as it was in 1600. By 2024 it will have
> slumped to the same level as it was in the
> Dark Ages.

Appleyard goes on to draw the only conclusion possible: "Almost daily, new evidence is emerging that progress can no longer be taken for granted, that a new Dark Age is lying in wait for ourselves and our children."

So that's it, really: the oil's run out, the climate's going to get hotter/colder and we are now officially too stupid to come up with any credible solutions. Before you throw the book down and run into the street screaming: "Oh my God, what are we going to do!", let me offer you a few crumbs of comfort. I do happen to know quite a bit about the first Dark Ages, and I think this might prove useful.

The Dark Ages mark a period of about 200 to 300 years immediately after the fall of the Roman Empire. When they start really depends upon where you are. Although 476 is traditionally regarded as the year the empire fell, it didn't disappear overnight. In Britain, for example, the Dark Ages mark the period between about AD 400 – when the Roman legions began to leave and southern Britain was dominated by a Latin-speaking, Christian, Romanised landowning class – and about AD 600, when the Anglo-Saxons started to write things down and history started again.

The Dark Ages are so called not because we were fighting orcs, or searching for the Holy Grail, but because nobody today knows what happened. It's like a journey, where we can see the starting point and the destination, but have no idea how we got from A to B. In AD 400 the population was relatively urbanised, living in towns in tenements made of brick, stone, concrete and tile, under a centralised government which raised taxes that were paid using minted coins. This revenue was spent on roads, public buildings and, most importantly, a vast standing army.

In the countryside, the ruling classes lived in centrally heated villas and dedicated their spare time to the nuances of Latin grammar and writing poems to their friends. Goods were manufactured and sold commercially and there was trade across an empire that stretched from Hadrian's Wall to the River Euphrates. There were grammar schools, public baths and economic production.

When history begins again in AD 600 we find a very different picture. This Romanised class has disappeared; gone too are their tenements and villas, while economic production has virtually ceased altogether. Most goods are now produced at home rather than bought commercially.

The population has massively declined, coins are no longer used for exchange, towns have disappeared and brick and stone buildings have been replaced with wattle-and-daub huts. There are virtually no buildings above two storeys high.

The old imperial provinces have been replaced by twenty or more small kingdoms that owe nothing to the political geography of the empire. We may not know *how* it happened but we do know *what* happened: typical British lifestyles rapidly disappeared as soon as the legions left.

So the Dark Ages happened because the Romans left. And the Romans left because the empire went into decline. And the empire went into decline because … well, for a great many reasons, but the important thing to remember is that it didn't happen because the Romans had stopped inventing things.

I can only speak for myself, but it's going to take a little bit more than "elaborate mathematics" to get me moving out of my centrally heated home into a wattle-and-daub bijou abode. Just because things aren't getting better as fast as they were doesn't mean we are going to abandon our iPods in favour of lutes. Embourgeoisement is a late-twentieth-century phenomenon. You only have to go back three or four generations to find that most people who were poor stayed poor. They would be living in conditions that would have been recognisable to ancestors visiting from hundreds of years ago. Things might not be getting better as quickly as they once were, but that doesn't mean they are necessarily going to get worse. The claim is simply the latest in a series of apocalypse scenarios going all the way back to Malthus's *Essay on Population*, through Soviet invasion plans and the coming Ice Age to the Millennium Bug and Moore's Law. I'll no doubt be eating my words when the Saxon longboats arrive, but at least the Internet won't be around for Bryan Appleyard to email me a smug "I told you so" missive.*

---

* For more on the subject of Moore's Law, see *City Slackers*.

I'm not saying that Appleyard's prediction is definitely utter nonsense, but I am saying I'll be amazed if it isn't.*

Every day, acres of media coverage are dedicated to future gazing. Whole industries, and not just the obvious ones like finance, banking and gambling, are built upon trying to guess what will happen next.

The irony is, we're just so bad at it. Experts are no better at predicting the outcome of events than rank amateurs. How many pundits – I wonder – have ever won the football pools? And don't kid yourself that scientists or economists are any better at it than footballers. Ronald Reagan allegedly relied on the advice from an official astrologer before making important decisions, and no doubt felt reassured to find that "Today, money matters will be important to you, Mr President ..."

But you have to wonder whether he would have fared any better had he been listening to the "real" experts who told subsequent presidents that "tech stocks are the future", "there is no such thing as global warming" and "take no notice of Hans Blix – honestly, that Saddam Hussein has got loads of weapons".

Despite the fact that most of us don't know what's going to happen this afternoon, the number of books, TV programmes and newspaper articles dedicated to predicting with absolute certainty what is going to happen

---

* Still, if you're the sort of person who was hiding in their cellar, surrounded by bottled water and tinned meat, while the rest of us were partying because it was 1999, then I can recommend Bryan Appleyard's *Understanding the Present*, a polemical attack on science that allows you to do anything but. Chock full of laughs it isn't.

tomorrow is staggering. The one thing they all have in common is that they are all wrong: it's just that some will end up being more wrong than others.

All future gazing firmly belongs in the category of science fiction. That's not to say it's not interesting or thought-provoking, and it does provide good discussion currency; but ultimately, you've got to remember, it is all bollocks. History doesn't repeat itself and we can't predict the future.

This is not a book about the future, it's about the present, and specifically about why the present isn't as good as it should be. This, I believe, owes an enormous amount to our inability to admit we really can't see into the future and as such we should stop wasting our time trying.

This disappointment and dissatisfaction with 21st-century-life in the West is widespread. True, historically most people have lived relatively short lives of abject misery, but today there seems little excuse to be unhappy.

My jet-pack fantasy is not unique. Many people were affected by them. Erstwhile Pulp lead singer Jarvis Cocker claimed that as a child he was so swayed by their apparently imminent introduction he never bothered learning how to ride a bike.

As late as 1985, the WASP II was featured in Jane's *All the World's Aircraft*, but as soon as the US military lost interest, development funds dried up and attempts to market it commercially under the name X-Jet failed. Even the 30 minutes of flight time were too limited for commercial purposes. The company still receives calls from would-be jet-pack pilots on a regular basis, but is sadly rather embarrassed about the WASP II and its predecessors.

While I was writing this I managed to track down some of the short films made of test flights (is there anything not online these days?). Flying a jet pack still looks just as amazing as it did 30 years ago, and I still want one more that ever. There is clearly a demand, but nowhere in the world will you find anyone seriously engaged in jet-pack development today.

For the (return of) the Dark Ages contingent, this is symptomatic of the problems with innovation. They believe there are only two reasons why we no longer witness the great leaps forward that defined the nineteenth and twentieth centuries: either we have run out of things to discover, or the process of thinking up new ideas has become too difficult.

Huebner and Appleyard are wrong. People are innovating as much as they ever have, it's just that their efforts are focused in different areas, areas that won't necessarily reward their thinking with patents. The people who would normally be doing the innovating are busy simply doing other things.

The world no longer needs jet-pack inventors, it needs people to run focus groups, to launch brand extensions, to conduct telemarketing campaigns, to present radio phone-ins, to develop new ways of processing what was once perfectly good food, to publish the *Daily Mail*, to produce reality TV shows, to dream up new flavours of crisp, to vote for singers with the X factor, to do degrees in media studies, to interview Westlife, to conceive viral marketing initiatives, to design a website for Cillit Bang, to persuade grown women to walk around with an obscene typo on their chest, to work in product marketing, to dedicate their lives to adding shareholder value, to take pictures for *Nuts* magazine, to put together compilation CDs for Starbucks, to write a blog about a video game, to sell ready meals, to do the Atkins diet, to pay attention to Simon Cowell, to programme a novel piece of software for a mobile phone, to work out to a Jade Goody DVD, to settle down in front of *Most Haunted*, to get "quoted happy", to be interested in *What Sadie Did Next*, to eat at KFC, to kit their houses out with IKEA furniture, to take a homoeopathic cure, to get with a new-wave religion, to live in urban apartments, to have their loyalty card with them, to buy one, get one free, to "maybe start with TV presenting, but then move into acting", to use the phrases "big time", "from day one" or "at the end of the day" in an interview situation, to read a Katie Price novel she's not even written, to become management consultants, to tune into Chris Moyles, to spam 4 billion people to see whether they want a penis enlargement, to check out that Queen musical Ben Elton wrote, to wonder what Prince Charles/Philip thinks about it, to buy an off-road vehicle for exclusively on-road purposes, to be excited by the free DVD that comes with the daily paper, to live a Lotto, to support a war on drugs/terror, to dine out at Frankie and Benny's, to get a spray-on tan, to attend a networking event, to write an article for *Grazia*, to take a lie-detector test live on daytime TV, to remortgage their house, to take a year out to broaden their mind, to buy a celebrity-endorsed light bulb, to believe that having a cup of hot chocolate in front of *Coronation Street* is better than an orgasm, to drink Australian wine, to ring up radio phone-in programmes to agree/disagree with an issue, to downsize, to worry whether they are suffering from one of "the seven signs of ageing", to pass off as their own opinion something they have been told by the media ...

One thing that ten-year-old me couldn't help noticing before he went back: the world in 2006 really is full of useless things.

## 3 | **Those Who Know Best**

*"Get up early … work hard … and strike oil."*
*John Paul Getty on the secret of his success*

In 1976 ten-year-old me often wished he had God-like powers. He spent a lot of time wondering what it would be like to fly, be invisible or even to have a serious car crash and have his puny human limbs replaced with bionics.

At junior school I was taught that the "real" or "one true" God was a benevolent all-knowing and all-powerful being: there was nothing that He couldn't do. I didn't find this fact particularly remarkable at the time. Clearly, if someone was able to create the whole world and everything in it in just six days (it's sometimes forgotten that he had a well-earned day off on the seventh), then the fact he could do what he liked and knew everything was, I supposed, pretty much to be expected. But my ears did prick up when I was told that not only was God infallible, but – for some reason I never understood – so was the Pope. Now in the instance of the Pope, I was pretty keen to understand how this worked. God was … well, he was God, but the Pope, I was certain, started life as a pretty normal bloke. I realised I was unlikely to meet God in real life, or indeed come into contact with anyone who had, but the Pope was a different matter. He lived not all that far away in Italy, and we were both, I was pleased to discover, Roman Catholics. It was conceivable that if I put my mind to it we might one day get to hook up with the Big Guy's number-one representative on earth. And when we did, boy, did I have some interesting questions for him!

I couldn't wait around for an audience with the Pope for ever. In the interim, the closest I was going to get in the short term to God's Representative on Earth was Miss Darby, my RE teacher. Miss Darby had an amiable – one might almost say Anglican – God-is-love take on the Catholic faith, as opposed to, say, a more traditional Spanish Inquisition "Who made me? God made me! Why did he make me? To know and to love him!" standpoint.

Miss Darby played the acoustic guitar. A lot. And she told us stories about people finding God in unusual places. Often these places were very dark – such as concentration camps, gulags and prisons – but they were always inspirational. One thing we didn't really study with her, at least initially, was the Bible. But once a few of the more religiously inclined parents got wind of how we were being taught, there was evidently some coercion from the headmaster, and religious education became less about singing "Where Have All the Flowers Gone?" and more about good old-fashioned beating the love of God into us.

So it came to pass that we entered a world of venal and cardinal sin, of indulgences, catechisms, benediction, transubstantiation and the mystery of the mass. I'll admit, I was much happier singing "I will make you fishers of men" – at least, I was until Miss Derby mentioned this infallibility thing.

"Yes, Steven."

"Miss, does that mean the Pope gets everything right?"

"On matters of doctrine, it does, yes."

"So does that mean he never gets things wrong?"

"Of course it does – he is infallible, after all."

"So if he was on *Mastermind*, he'd, like, get every single question right?"

"Well, not quite. Anyway, he wouldn't use his God-given powers in such a vulgar way."

"And has he always been able to do this, or did it just happen when he became the Pope?"

"Only the Pope is infallible."

"So it's not like he's got a hundred per cent in every exam?"

"No, it's not like that."

"If you were thinking of a number, would he know what number it was?"

"That's enough of this nonsense, Steven. Turn to page 107 in your hymn books and we'll all sing 'Morning Has Broken'."

Today – again for reasons I don't really understand – the Pope is apparently no longer infallible. Ironically, the world is now dominated by people who think that they are.

Imagine for a moment that you are extremely rich and successful (I'm assuming you're probably not). In fact, let's imagine your career has made you so fabulously wealthy that money has ceased to have any real meaning to you. You can have whatever you want, whenever you want it.

Clearly, you don't believe there's anything intrinsically wrong with this. You've worked really hard and are simply enjoying the trappings of your achievement. Well done, you.

Now, let's also imagine that you are regularly inter-viewed by the media. Inevitably they always ask the same question: what is the secret of your success? You answer it the same way every time it comes up. You need talent obviously, but more humbly, you also believe it's down to having the courage to take difficult decisions when required and making the right decisions at the right time. At this point you pause for effect, before leaning towards the interviewer and adding with a wink, "And of course, you need a little bit of luck along the way."

The journalist laughs and you laugh. You both know that in this game you make your own luck.

At the top of the success tree, there's no manager to appraise your performance; in fact you'll get precious little feedback from anyone. Your staff may think you're a genius but they might also think you're an idiot. And you'll never know for sure which it is. Nobody will tell you you're wrong. If they do, the chances are they won't hang around very long.

Before long you'll have forgotten what it was like to be gainsaid or challenged at all. How hard would it be, then, to come to the conclusion that, if no one ever tells you you're wrong, then you must always be right? After all, look at how very successful you are. And it's all your brilliant ideas for new products, PR launches, marketing activity and company acquisitions that are driving the business forward. Or should that be into the ground?

Hubris is not a new concept – the Ancient Greeks knew a thing or two about it – but the opportunities to indulge in hubris have never been greater than they are today. Everybody's at it – just open a newspaper, turn on the TV, visit a store or, indeed, just go to work, and you'll find examples of hubris everywhere. You just have to know what you're looking for.

Every day the media is filled with news of announcements, projects and decisions that reek of hubris. It can be something as huge as the invasion of a foreign sovereign state without any legal auspices whatsoever or something more prosaic like the multi-million-pound launch of a new brand of bottled water without any understanding of the market at all. It could be something as trivial as a reality TV runner-up unsuccessfully trying to anchor a daytime satellite show about macramé or an album of swing classics from a popular performer who really ought to know better.

All it takes is a total lack of self-awareness combined with a perceived opportunity to make money. The common denominator is that the results will always be useless.

On 3 November 1997 the Spice Girls released their second album, *Spiceworld*. They were the biggest band on the planet, shipping 7 million copies in just fourteen days. Four days later, they decided to sack their creator and manager, Simon Fuller. "We feel in our hearts that this is the right decision for us," said the official statement from the band. "We would like our fans to know that we are positive and excited about the future."

The statement from Simon Fuller's company, 19 Management, was less mercurial: "This is very much the girls' idea and we wish them the very best of luck in the future ... They are five very talented, successful, motivated women who know what they want and Simon is a brilliant manager and the girls are now empowered to go on to new heights."

Alas, the girls soon found that there was more to this

management lark than there had appeared. While undoubtedly very good at dancing in time, singing in tune and saying "Girl power", the girls soon found that these skills were slightly less transferable to the business of tour management, sponsorship acquisition, financial planning, legalities, strategic marketing, promotional activity and licence negotiation. The stress soon got to them. Fights broke out and five became four when Geri Halliwell – whose resignation, allegedly, came as a great surprise to her – left in May of the following year.

The Spice Girls' difficult third album, *Forever* – so called presumably as a testament to how long it had taken to record – was eventually released in November 2000. It was a dreadful record and consequently had the life expectancy of a circus goldfish, peaking at a miserable number 39 in the United States, and achieving a fraction of the sales of its predecessors.

Success is very difficult to repeat. People who have struggled to succeed devote much of their time to removing what they perceive to be controlling influences. The Spice Girls sacked Fuller because he was too controlling, despite the fact that this control had been one of the biggest contributing factors to their success. Hubris takes over and drives people to believe that if only they could shake off these creative restraints, the product they are working on could be the best ever. Take heed from the example of unfettered girl power: all that happens is that quality control goes out the window.

Many senior managers – but MDs and CEOs in particular – suffer from hubris. They confuse being lucky with being a genius. They believe that their success is a direct result of their own choices and decisions and never take external factors into consideration.

Please be clear, I am not undermining people's achievements; what I am challenging is the belief that success is simply a recipe that can be repeated again and again and again. What people don't want to accept is that the quality of the decisions they made has as much to do with the environment they were taken in – the market conditions, the kinds of insights and messages they get, the activities of their customers and competitors, and the timing – and that these factors are incredibly difficult to duplicate. Location – in terms of being in the right place, at the right time – plays a huge role in determining success or failure, but most businesses don't fully understand, or accept, the contribution this makes to their competitive position.

It's not difficult to see how this state of affairs comes about. As a more specific example, imagine you are the owner/manager of a start-up telephone hygiene business. You visit clients at their offices in your own town, cleaning people's phones, and you make enough money to pay yourself a modest wage, but on the upside you are your own boss and you make all the decisions.

Then, one day, the *Daily Mail* runs an article which says a new study it has commissioned shows that it's possible to catch the MRSA virus, Aids and bird flu from a dirty telephone handset.*

Suddenly your small business is inundated with calls

---

* They inevitably go on to blame the government and asylum seekers, but that's not really relevant.

from worried *Daily Mail* readers. Work starts flooding in and you decide to expand. You soon realise you are the only business in the office-phone cleaning sector, so you find it easy to pick up big contracts. You take on even more staff, open a satellite office and role the business out nationally.

Three years later you are employing 600 people and turning over millions of pounds from the business of protecting the UK's office workers from the MRSA virus. You are looking at expanding into Europe. You've got other people running the business now so, with a little time on your hands, you decide to write a book about this crazy three-year rollercoaster called *Can You Hold Please? The Secret of My Success*.

Now here's the question: do you put all this success down to that one article in the *Daily Mail*?

Of course you don't.

As time goes on you decide to expand the business, by moving into a completely new area: something sexier like, say, cleaning computers. Now here's the other question: what on earth makes you think people are going to want to buy this service from you?

You've built your business up organically and flourished on the back of a lucky break. Launching a new venture on this scale is a completely different challenge. If you're smart, you'll realise this and buy in some expertise. Alternatively, you can say I've done it once, I can do it again. Who knows, maybe you'll be lucky twice.

Over the years I've probably worked with more than two hundred companies. These businesses have come in all shapes and sizes: from huge multinational banks and telecommunications businesses to small independent record labels and magazine publishers. Whether they've been launching a new national digital radio station or a limited-edition seven-inch single they all have one thing in common: none of them is as interesting as they think they are.

This is a forgivable excess: when it becomes dangerous is when companies start believing they are much better than they really are. It's from these businesses I start running.

Company histories are exactly like the Dark Ages. We know where the business started and we pretty much know where it is today, but don't let anyone kid you they know how it got there. Companies can rarely say with any certainty what their share price will be in three months' time. What is less well known is that they are usually just as uncertain about what actually happened in the past.

Company histories and case studies are useless because they are written backwards with the benefit of hindsight. Starting with the outcome, they extrapolate, working out how they must have solved each problem they came across in reverse. It's a bit like being helicoptered on to the top of a mountain and then working out how you might have got there had you climbed up it.

There is no necessary correlation between success and performance or between success and quality. Just because you're successful or popular doesn't necessarily mean you're performing well or producing quality. In fact being successful doesn't necessarily mean you're any good at all.

"But Steve, a million people can't be wrong, can they?" I hear you cry. Well, I dunno, ask the million or so people who bought *Be Here Now* the day it came out.

## 4 | **White Elephant Gods**

*Positively Happy: Cosmic Ways to Change*
*Your Life*
      by Noel Edmonds, TV presenter

Back in 1976, the muse within the ten-year-old me was awakening what was to become a lifelong obsession with music. At this early stage in my taste-forming development, I was pretty catholic (sorry!) in my musical choices. Every morning, I had my breakfast while listening to Noel Edmonds on the Radio 1 breakfast show, and every evening I had my dinner listening to Dave Lee Travis on the drive-time show.

Dave Lee Travis – or DLT – was, at this innocent time, by far and away my favourite Radio 1 DJ. DLT was born in Derbyshire in 1945. Beginning his career as an interior designer, he got his break in music at the age of nineteen when he toured America with Herman's Hermits. In the UK he hosted his own show on Radio Caroline for two and a half years until the ship was blown aground in early 1965.

After a stint as a TV presenter in West Germany, he joined the BBC in 1967 shortly after the launch of Radio 1. And it was at Radio 1 that he stayed for the next 25 years.

By 1976 Travis was a huge star. Radio 1 was less than ten years old and the concept of the DJ – at this time the more formal disc jockey was still in common usage – was a relatively new one in Britain. The drive-time show I enjoyed listening to was *It's DLT OK!*, which he launched in 1975. In 1978 he was chosen to anchor Radio 1's flag-ship breakfast show.* The reach that this gave DLT into the nation's homes is almost inconceivable in today's frag-mented digital media landscape. There was scant competi-tion from commercial radio and no breakfast TV. As a result, 15 million people were tuning into DLT's show on a daily basis. He was waking up the nation.

It's fair to say I grew up with DLT. Our relationship began with unironic admiration on my part. At the time, I thought he was hilarious. Self-consciously wacky with a penchant for funny voices.†

Travis was larger than life, and can be considered the founder of the "You don't have to be mad to work here – but it helps!" school of comedy. DLT would not think twice about using now-taboo words like "zany" or "madcap" to describe his live-on-air antics: "Anything can happen and probably will." Even though, in reality, it never did.

I recall that he once played the wrong record and reacted

---

* To coincide with his move to the breakfast show he changed his nickname from "The Hairy Monster" to "The Hairy Cornflake". Do you see what he did there?

† Nothing exciting – the usual casual racism that was considered harmless (by the white establishment) at the time, e.g. a Daft Taffy, Naive Jamaican or Thrifty Jock. But don't judge him: this was the 1970s, a time when Johnny Foreigner provided nearly all the laughs. As a nation we chuckled to *Love Thy Neighbour*, *Mind Your Language* and *The Comedians* and sang along with the Black and White Minstrels, and when we weren't making gags about them going into pubs with Scotsmen and Englishmen, we were wont to lock up anyone with an Irish accent, but only after giving them a bloody good kicking. Not so much more innocent as pig-ignorant and nastier times.

as if Prince Charles had walked into the studio juggling kittens with their hair on fire.

He was a fan of comedic devices like malapropism. The likes of Gloria Estefan and Terence Trent Darby became Glorious Extractor Fan and Terence Trent Water Authority. Laydees – and they were always laydees, never wimmin – were invariably lovely: "'Lilac Wine' there from Elkie Brooks: beautiful laydee, beautiful voice."

DLT was big on audience participation. Regular treats included the Tranogram, the Dreaded Cringe and the Think Link – for which we were invited to "think laterally". Correct answers would be rewarded with a Radio 1 Goody Bag, incorrect answers by his trademark "Quack! Quack! Oops!" sound effect. This reached a high point with the unlikely concept of a snooker-on-the radio quiz, "Give Us a Break".

As I got older I began to realise that beneath the studied lunacy there was a darker side to DLT. His phenomenal ego displayed itself in occasional on-air outbursts about the populist issues of the day. Seal-clubbing (anti), nurses' pay (pro) and inconsiderate drivers (anti) all came under his analytical microscope. His ruminations were at best glaringly obvious platitudes: "So remember, in fog – it's foot off the gas! Got it?", but more often showed a jaw-dropping lack of understanding about the wider economic issues affecting the conservation of fishing stocks in Labrador, Canada.

> Most of you are having your breakfast now,
> and if you feel you might be put off by what

> I'm about to say, please turn off the radio for
> a few minutes … seals [are] being culled … if
> you have a newspaper in your house, there's a
> piece of paper looking for your signature,
> saying, "We don't want this any more."

Despite being a DJ, Travis famously wasn't into music. John Peel once visited his house and was amazed to see that Travis didn't have any records: "Too much trouble, too much dust," the Hairy One told him. In his defence, I do vividly recall an impassioned plea he made once to "any record company bods who may be listening in" to get "Elkie Brooks and Chris Rea together in the studio. They may not get on, but I for one would love to hear what they come up with and I'm not alone."

Away from the radio, Travis's extra-curricular activities, in terms of highly lucrative personal appearances, were enough to keep him in slippers. My colleague Nick Bax provides this eyewitness account of a DLT PA from 1979.*

> I remember Dave Lee Travis once visited the
> Yorkshire village of Maltby, my former home
> town, one Sunday lunchtime to open a brand-
> new housing estate. He arrived in a

---

* For those of you who are interested in the subject of celebrities opening housing estates in Maltby, Nick also recalls the visit in 1979 of Red Rum. "Rummy" opened a show house for Tarmac Homes (on the road behind the Bax family's new bungalow). He left a hoof print in a concrete slab set into the front garden, which is still there to this day.

chauffeur-driven white Rolls-Royce, accompanied by a blonde bimbo who might have been a member of Legs & Co. I can't be sure.

DLT was immaculately clad in a coat of fur that was colour-coordinated with his beard. I don't think it was made from baby seals, more likely from animals lower down the love-list – mink perhaps? As I recall he was considerably less enthusiastic about this personal appearance than me and my schoolmates were. He began by asking the master of ceremonies exactly how long all this was going to take and then egregiously warned us to keep away from the car. Then he had his photo taken, and fucked off. He can't have been there for any more than fifteen minutes. At no point in the proceedings was he more than four paces away from the car.*

---

* This is slightly irrelevant but I thought you might be interested. Nick also confirmed that high-speed personal appearances of this kind were by no means atypical. His best friend's mum could stake a reasonable claim to being Rotherham's most famous traffic warden. One day she was fortunate enough to catch sight of Noel Edmonds, then at the height of his *Swap Shop* pomp, when he opened a jewellery shop – possibly a branch of Ratners, possibly not – directly opposite her house. In fact, lucky is not the word. She had not intended to catch Noel, and indeed was unaware that he was due to open the shop at all, having just simply popped home for lunch. She arrived at the gate in full uniform just as a large motor car – which may or may not have been a Jag – pulled up at the kerb. "You can't park there," she yelled, failing to recognise the goateed driver.

A minor moment in what was, by anyone's standards, a glittering career. Which is why it's so amazing that today, 30 years on, DLT's cultural legacy is zero. You'll find precious little about him on the Internet, he's never been the subject of a retrospective, a biography or a TV documentary, and his body of work is unlikely ever to be re-evaluated. An unscientific, but still rather telling, straw poll among the account managers at work (80 per cent female, average age 24, all Radio 1 listeners) showed that nobody surveyed had ever heard of him.

This is largely due to the circumstances of his departure from the BBC. It was an act that demonstrates just how dangerous hubris can be. Travis resigned in the summer of 1993. A new Radio 1 controller, Matthew Bannister, had been appointed, but was yet to take over officially. It was no secret that Bannister's remit was to shake things up. In 1993, Radio 1, which was nominally the BBC's youth flagship, had an audience whose average age was 31. To attract a younger audience, Bannister and his new head of music, Trevor Dann, decided they were going to have to put music at the heart of the Radio 1 offer. They also realised that in order for this strategy to succeed they were

---

Edmonds gave the textbook celebrity riposte: "Don't you know who I am?" "No I bloody don't. And you're not parking there." Noel rallied brilliantly – he had no interest in arguing. "Honestly, I'll only be two minutes," he said. He turned, waited briefly for an appropriate gap in the traffic, and sprinted across the road, where he shook the hand of the store manager, posing for a quick photo, before cutting the ribbon and sprinting back to his car. Just before he sped off he winked and said: "Five seconds to spare, love!" Which, all in all, makes DLT's fifteen minutes look like quite good value.

going to have to transfer a sizeable proportion of Radio 1's existing audience to Radio 2.

The old guard DJs like Travis, Simon "Our Tune" Bates and that master of the single entendre Gary "Bit in the Middle" Davies were seen as the root of most of these problems.

The smarter DJs understood this. Steve Wright – not short on ego himself – quietly announced that he was moving to Radio 2, and simply took his popular zoo-format show and its listeners to a different frequency. In light of this, you might think that DLT would simply follow suit, take matters into his own hands and jump before he was pushed: bowing out honourably, with dignity intact.

Oh no!

He announced his resignation live on air: "Changes are being made here that go against my principles and I really just want to put the record straight and thought that you ought to know first." He went on to rail about Bannister – who had not even started in office – to any journalist who'd listen, in a move that Andy Parfitt, then chief assistant to the Controller at Radio 1, called "the laugh of the century".

But the snow-capped peak on Ego Mountain was surely when he aligned himself with the Herculean BBC World Service reporter, Sir Mark Tully.

Tully was the BBC's legendary India correspondent. He has won countless awards for his investigative journalism in a brilliant 40-year career. He's dodged bullets on the India–Pakistan border, movingly described the crippling effects of absolute poverty on Calcutta's child street beggars, and was the first Western journalist to get to grips with the Bhopal chemical disaster. It is difficult to sum up his dazzling career in a couple of paragraphs, but in short, Tully is almost single-handedly responsible for transforming our understanding of the subcontinent.

He also happened to resign from the BBC World Service – where, coincidentally, DLT had a request show – in protest against what he saw as senior management's abandonment of its public service ethos around the same time the Hairy Cornflake was deciding to announce his departure from Radio 1. DLT explains:

> What happened was Mark Tully had done
> this from the far end of the spectrum, where
> nary a Radio 1 listener would dare to tread.
> "Who's Mark Tully?" they'd probably say ...
>
> ... They've got Mark Tully here and right at
> the other end [of the spectrum] is Dave Lee
> Travis. The press thinks, "Now there must be
> a story."*

They didn't. They thought, "Here must be two completely unrelated stories."

There's no denying that Travis had a very successful career, but he had precious little talent. He substituted ego for talent, and got away with it because his daytime radio

---

* Dave Lee Travis interview in Simon Garfield, *The Nation's Favourite, the True Adventures of Radio 1*, Faber & Faber, 1998.

peers were pretty much doing the same. But when the rules of the game changed, he lacked the self-awareness to realise the weakness of his position and led a Canute-like, one-man protest against the changes to his Wonderful World of Radio 1. Anyone with a lesser ego would have been able to see the weakness of their position; in the event, his on-air railings against "The Man" meant he'd burnt more bridges than Napoleon on his retreat from Moscow.

The timing of his resignation was nonsense: he was due to leave anyway, as his contract had less than three months to run. Second, he offered his services to Radio 2 only after his outburst. His performances over the final few years on Radio 1 were exercises in studied mediocrity: the epitome of somebody going through the motions. Innovation was anathema; DLT refused to move with the times, stoically sticking to his guns. One on-air outburst in 1989 concerned the Cookie Crew, a UK female rap duo, and their single "Got to Keep On", which features a sample from soul legend Edwin Starr. Travis started playing the record only to cut the track after about 45 seconds. Clearly irritated and sounding dangerously close to a "I'm not a racist but ..." stance, the Hairy One explained his actions: "I'm sorry. I've got nothing against this rap music, but that's just stealing! Now here's a real record."

He then played Starr's 1969 hit "25 Miles": the track from which the offending sample was taken. This one moment encapsulated everything that was wrong with Radio 1: egotistic, overblown, anachronistic and pig ignorant. The only surprise is that it took four years to put it right.

Radio 2 politely declined Travis's offer, and with that DLT disappeared from the national consciousness for ever.

Hubris grows from success, and this combination always leads to mediocrity. In the case of DLT, providence was the major factor in his success. His "talent", like that of Happy in *Death of a Salesman*, was to be well liked. But even when a career is built on real talent, hubris is still capable of acting as a corruptive force, turning the great into the useless.

Take the career of the undeniably talented actor John Travolta. Here's my version of John Travolta's biography done straight from memory with no research or reference material. See how it compares with your own.

Travolta starred in *Grease* and *Saturday Night Fever* in the late 1970s and became the biggest star on the planet. After that, he kind of disappeared for a while. I recall he did an unsuccessful follow-up to *Saturday Night Fever* called *Stayin' Alive* in the early 1980s, and turned up again towards the decade's end in the romantic comedy *Look Who's Talking*. He may or may not have appeared in the sequels.

At some point during this period he became a Scientologist. And that would have been that, had not Quentin Tarantino had the foresight to cast him as wise guy Vincent Vega in his brilliant 1994 film *Pulp Fiction*. Travolta put in the performance of his career, and we all ordered a "Royale with cheese" the next time we visited McDonald's by way of homage. Once again he's the biggest star on the planet. He gets $20 million to appear in *Face/Off* and puts in another sterling performance in the movie *Get Shorty*.

Everything falls apart in 2000, when he spends $73 million of his own money on a screen version of Scientology founder L. Ron Hubbard's novel *Battlefield Earth*. After that it's a bit quiet.

So in a nutshell, a career of highs and hiatuses of comedowns and comebacks currently in one of its fallow periods, but given the amount of money he's made, I don't feel we should be wasting our worry beads on him.

Unsurprisingly, Travolta has a very different view of his success. In February 2006 an interviewer put it to him that:

> He's had more comebacks than the proverbial
> boomerang, so much so, he's been dubbed
> The Comeback Kid but ask John Travolta
> what he makes of his yo-yo career and he
> looks genuinely bemused.
>
> "You know what I was never aware of it," he
> says. "Kirstie Alley, who I worked with, told
> everyone that I was never aware of having
> cooled off and it's true. Until I got hired for
> *Pulp Fiction* I didn't know I had cooled off."*

Let's put that one down to self-confidence, but how about this, from an interview in 1999 about his role in *Pulp Fiction*: "I'd like to say I was the hero who saved *Pulp Fiction*."†

---

* Tiscali.co.uk, 24 February 2006.
† Well-rounded.com, June 1999.

In his mind, it was his performance which made *Pulp Fiction*, not the film which jump-started his ailing career. In 2004 he was interviewed by BBC's Tom Brook.*

> *Tom Brook*: "What about *Battlefield Earth*? Do you feel that that was a mistake?"
>
> *John Travolta*: "No, I would do it over again right away, I love that movie and I love the book, and I'm very proud that I got to do it. It was using my power and doing what I wanted to do."
>
> *Tom Brook*: "Do you think people were wrong for criticising that film?"
>
> *John Travolta*: "Well, you know, everyone has their right to do whatever, but I've been in other films that were far worse criticised than that. That was actually liked and loved by Lucas and Tarantino and a lot of people I love and respect. It was actually in the higher end of admiration than most."

You probably haven't seen *Battlefield Earth*. Take it from me, life is too short. Here's what Amazon has to say about the DVD.

> In the 30th Century, when *Battlefield Earth* is uncovered in a mass grave for bad films by

---

* BBCWorld.com, December 2004.

revisionist cineastes, it is more than likely that it will *still* be the worst science fiction film ever made. John Travolta's $73m pet sci-fi project – an adaptation of Scientology guru L Ron Hubbard's rambling pulp novel – is like the long lost sequel to Ed Wood's *Plan Nine from Outer Space*. Incompetent, incomprehensible and, at nearly two hours running time, way over long, *Battlefield Earth* is nothing more than a rehash of hackneyed post-*Star Wars* sci-fi clichés.

It's time to stop picking on John, he's by no means unique. Here's another example from the Z-end of the celebrity alphabet. During Christmas 2005, the BBC ran a series of *Celebrity Mastermind*. The format was exactly the same as normal *Mastermind*, except the questions were put to "famous" people rather than members of the public.

One of the contestants – whose occupation was given as "classical pianist" – was Mylene Klass. Now we've all been a bit creative on our CVs from time to time, but "classical pianist" really is stretching it a bit. What Mylene is famous for is winning *Popstars*, the first reality music business TV show (pre-Cowell in fact), and as a result joining briefly famous chart-toppers and apostrophe criminals Hear'Say. "Wannabe Reality TV Show Moppet" might be a more accurate description of her occupation.

Mylene is an applause junkie masquerading as a classical pianist. Not for her the years of painstaking practice, dedication and effort to gain one of the few places to study at one of the greatest colleges in the world, followed by years of penury, living an ascetic lifestyle, while attempting to carve out a career as a struggling musician. No, siree, she's taken the non-typical route of taking part in a reality TV show and being relatively easy on the eye. Classical musicians are surely born, not made. A passion for music, and a willingness to sacrifice almost anything to continually improve your performance, is, I'm pretty certain, a prerequisite for success in the job. I'm not sure it's something you can "have a crack at" if all else fails, or even fall back on if things don't work out.

Here's a review of her 2003 debut album, *Moving On*:

> To an untrained ear they might sound impressive but if anyone has heard the originals they will notice instantly that her adaptations aren't half as good. In particular I was horrified at Toccata and Fugue where the same segment of music was played over and over repetitively. One of Bach's greatest works was reduced to a cacophony of noise, not unlike Chopsticks.*

I can only imagine that her decision to appear on *Celebrity Mastermind* was an ideal opportunity to position herself as an intelligent musician with her new target market. You can just imagine the conversation in the publicist's office, can't you?

---

* Amazon.co.uk, 8 November 2004.

"We've got the opportunity to do telly. Lots of eyeballs over the Crimble period and a great crossover opportunity for us. Lots of the dullards who tune into *Mastermind* are bound to like all that classical shit you do. Get revising, Mylene, you've been booked!"

For the Beeb, this was undoubtedly an attempt to broaden the appeal of its deliberately high-brow BBC2 quiz. Given that it was scheduled on BBC1, I wondered whether they were going to make the questions easier. I needn't have worried – John Humphrys didn't let me down.

So what specialist subject did Mylene choose to answer questions on, then? The Life and Works of Edvard Grieg? The influence of Baroque on Eighteenth-century Music? The Operas of Giacomo Puccini?

No.

Mylene's specialist subject was Series 3 of *Sex and the City*. That's right.

Not even *Sex and the City*, just Series 3. Or to put it another way: around twelve hours of television.

Unsurprisingly, at the end of the specialist subject round, Mylene was way out in front, with the series' first-ever maximum, a score of 18.

"It's a good job the buzzer went," said John Humphrys with no sign of irony, "I've run out of questions!"

The nation wondered how anyone could possible follow up this intellectual tour de force: the highest ever score on *Mastermind*. Something pretty amazing was going to have to happen in the general knowledge round if anyone was to top that. It was a wonder her fellow competitors didn't just give up and go home.

Fortunately Mylene had some entertainment aces up her sleeve. Not content with getting the highest score ever in round one, she went on to get the lowest score ever recorded for round two, answering only one question correctly.

"You passed on twelve," said John with no sign of a smile, keeping Mylene in her seat for what must have seemed an eternity to "Miss Bottom of the Klass", while he went through the answers. Ms Klass smiled, nodded, "ah yessed" and "of coursed" like the trouper she undoubtedly is before leaving to presumably fire her publicist.

That's if she can spell "fire", the big thicko!

Her public humiliation could easily have been avoided if only someone had had the temerity to say something along the lines of: "*Mastermind* – you have to be really smart to go on that, don't you?", or even "What's your general knowledge like?"

Intellectually speaking, Hollywood actress Jessica Simpson is widely regarded as being no cure for cancer, but that didn't stop her comparing herself to William Shakespeare when she was in the UK in 2005 to promote her role in Ibsen's *Hedda Gable*r at the National ... No, sorry, I meant her role as Daisy Duke in *The Dukes of Hazzard* movie: "When I arrived in England the first thing I did was go straight to the Globe Theatre. For me that is the home of acting and writing. As a writer myself, I have always loved Shakespeare. That's the job I want – anything at the Globe."*

---

* Radio Five Live interview, 24 August 2005.

I feel Jessica should set her sights slightly lower – like trying to eclipse the literary career of Naomi Campbell, whose 1994 potboiler *Swan* was eclipsed in the non-starter stakes only by her album *Babywoman* for Epic Records the following year. Both items marked the beginning and the end of her respective careers, leaving critics to ask the question: is there no beginning to her talent?*

The point is, most celebrities and senior managers never have their judgement questioned in this way. Constantly suggesting that your boss might have got this one wrong is a good strategy only if you want to get fired. Supporting their decisions is what you're paid to do, not gainsaying them. So think about it – if no one ever tells you you're wrong, you must always be right.

My friend worked for a large technology company and the CEO liked to tell jokes. Jokes aren't funny. They are generally told by people who aren't funny, who use the jokes to disguise the fact they've got no sense of humour. When the CEO told jokes at office get-togethers or on company golf days with major suppliers, everybody laughed. This state of affairs would have been fine, but he also told jokes in meetings with customers or on evenings out at trade events in the company of competitors. He really couldn't understand why his material wasn't working on these occasions.

People who behave hubristically are without insight.

---

* Again my view is probably not shared by Naomi. With what can only be described as a Stalinist approach to history, her US management, Associated Entertainment Consultants, describe *Swan* as an international bestseller. So there!

The process demands a complete lack of self-awareness, making them absolutely oblivious to the reaction their behaviour solicits. This reaction usually takes the form of jaw-dropping astonishment.

Hubris is not exclusive to celebrities or social occasions. Hubris also drives the development of products, is what makes reality TV shows so interesting, creates Z-list celebrities, and is responsible for bad books, bad films, bad TV and ultimately bad lives.

You don't have to look hard for examples of corporate hubris. The bargain bins of music stores or the remaindered sections of bookshops are a good place to start. Eighty per cent of new products fail, and of course they fail for many different reasons, but if you've ever looked at something and wondered, "How could anyone ever imagine people would want to buy that?" then it's probably hubris at work.

Senior managers, as I have said, confuse being lucky with being brilliant. Success does not breed success as often as it breeds complacency. The number of strategic decisions companies have to make today would stagger the entrepreneurs of the 1960s and 1970s. Flexibility, everyone will tell you, is absolutely critical to sustaining a successful business, and they're right. But it's so much easier to do what we did yesterday again today.

A surprising number of CEOs drive product development. They are names that dominate their respective trade papers, making bold pronouncements about the future of their markets. In most cases they have absolutely no idea what's going on among their own customers.

Film and music companies are generally run by lawyers and accountants, not people with a passion for film or music. Few CEOs of video games companies spend any of their spare time having a quick bash at Grand Theft Auto, despite blathering to the contrary in the specialist media. How many TV execs, I wonder, spend their evenings slumped in front of *Big Brother* or *Most Haunted*?

Bruno Bonnell is the flamboyant and eminently quotable CEO of video games publisher Atari. Despite several attempts to break into the top level, spending several hundred million euros in the process, Atari remains resolutely on the periphery. Indeed, in Atari's 20-year history, it's difficult to think of five seminal titles the company has developed.*

Yet if you read an interview with Bonnell, you'd be forgiven for thinking you were talking to the video games equivalent of Orson Welles or Francis Ford Coppola. Bonnell insists that all his company's games began with the legend "Bruno Bonnell Presents", the first and still the only CEO to do this. What Bruno was normally presenting was a piece of ill-conceived mediocrity – often with some movie licence tie-in to help paper over the chasms. Still, none of this has stopped him talking as if he invented the entire medium. Here's what he had to say about the future of video games in 2004:

---

* Without looking, I could only come up with: Driver, Alone in the Dark, Unreal Tournament and V-Rally. Even that last one is stretching things a bit.

In the past, game designers have viewed making their creations as something like producing an opera ... they want to produce something epic, titles that offer 30–40 hours of in-depth (and sometimes open-ended) play. Consumers are moving towards a desire for something more complete, and more exciting. It's as if they want to make the move from opera into pop music.

A new generation of consumers is growing that wants quick, fast-paced entertainment that's instantly gratifying. After all, dancing along to a pop song is more fun than watching a three-hour opera, isn't it? The problem is that in the past, the critics in our game industry have largely been opera specialists. This is going to change going forward.*

It's a nice image – moving from opera to pop music – and it's easy to understand, and on first listening it seems to make sense. In fact it's nothing more than the blathering of a man who has no affinity with his audience. A trite sound-bite sold to a willing interviewer.

Bonnell's strategy is doomed to failure. The reason his games don't sell as many as he'd like is probably because they're not very good. They don't need to be shorter, just better.

---

* Scott Steinberg, Oneup.com, 13 September 2004.

The bestselling games are usually works of genius – they sell millions because they give countless hours of entertainment and have the ability to engage and captivate.*

In February 2006, after a disastrous final quarter, Bonnell was engaged in an opera of his own. Atari issued a profits warning, showing a net loss of $5 million. The bad news was compounded by the departure of CFO Diane Baker, plus confirmation that HSBC had cut off its credit line. Media reports of "Game Over for Atari" swiftly followed.† People simply didn't want to buy Atari's pop pap. Unless he and his company pull their collective creative finger out, words are the only contribution he'll be making to the future itself. But it doesn't augur well. Bruno can pontificate about the future of video games all he likes – in all his years at the helm he's never been involved with a single title of lasting significance.

Hubris gives its sufferers the licence to inflict their creative barrel scrapings upon us. Should it disappear, the world won't miss Atari and its operettas; it has survived without DLT's think link; it will be able to sleep until Mylene Klass's next album is released; and it prefers to remember the "Royale with cheese" rather than Travolta's later fromage most royal.

Hubris has even become a religion itself. It's called the Cosmic Ordering Service. Basically the premise is this: you make a list of all the things you want, like a lottery windfall or your own hit TV series, pop it in an envelope and

---

* I'll admit, I'm a big video game fan.
† Lisa Foster, "Atari plans studio sell-off", MCV, 17 February 2006.

stick it under your pillow. Just leave the rest to the Cosmic Orderer – like an intergalactic QVC. Now even the Scientologists are tapping their temples, but the religion does have its celebrity subscribers. Noel Edmonds is a big believer. He attributes the success of his cult guessing game *Deal or No Deal* entirely to a kind of "two for one" offer he asked for from the Cosmic Ordering Service. When he was interviewed on *Parkinson* about it, the audience and host sat in mute disbelief. Edmonds gave the most chilling performance on-screen anyone has witnessed since somebody said, "No, Mr Bond, I expect you to die!"

At the time, along with a couple of million other viewers, I felt the hairs on the back of my neck stand up as the chilling realisation that he actually believed this shit began to hit me. Now, with the benefit of hindsight, I realise that Noel was only looking for a rational explanation, for why a goateed, has-been prankster with absolutely no sense of humour, talent or charisma could have relaunched his career in such a major way from such a minor daytime quiz slot. I don't know about you, but now I'm writing a list, and I'm checking it twice.

But we can't lay all the blame for all the useless things at the feet of those with unfettered egos. This may come as some surprise, but we're as much to blame as they are.

## Part Two | **Ignorance**

"Not ignorance, but ignorance of ignorance is the death of knowledge."

*Alfred North Whitehead,*
*mathematician and philosopher*

## 5 | **Science Fiction**

"No one ever went broke underestimating the intelligence of the American public."

*P. T. Barnum, showman*

I've got news for you: you're a thicko. I can understand it if you're now feeling slightly insulted, but believe me, it's true. I don't want you to take this the wrong way, though, so if it's any consolation, you're not on your own. I'm a thicko as well – we all are.

We may well be educating almost half the population to degree standard, but the inescapable truth is that we're still a very gullible bunch, ignorant not only of how the world about us works and functions, but moreover completely unaware that this knowledge might actually be important.

Collectively, we'll believe almost anything we're told, and we know very little that is of any practical use. We're very knowledgeable when it comes to the fluctuating weight and fortunes of minor celebrities, the personality traits determined by particular star signs, the colours of the season or even Arsenal's chances in the Champions League, but ask most of us a direct question about how something works and we'll be floundering like Mylene Klass in a game of *Trivial Pursuit*.

This lack of understanding makes it incredibly easy to sell us things.

We'll willingly sign on the line for any old crap, just as long as the snake-oil salesman has got their customer experience right and thrown some appropriately scientific-sounding patter into the mix.

In 1994 I was newly married and the proud co-owner of a dilapidated Edwardian terrace house. The bay window in the master bedroom needed replacing – the timber was completely rotten – and we decided that this should be the first job we would get sorted. We were quite naive when it came to hiring builders, but we knew that the done thing was to get three quotes and pick the one in the middle. The following evening, I received a cold call from Cold Seal, the double glazing people. They were offering a free quotation and 10 per cent off. How timely, I thought, and immediately booked a meeting with their qualified sales representative, much to the ill-disguised incredulity of the person on the other end of the phone.

The following evening, a man called Tom arrived with a big box of samples. He was new to the job, he told me, and so would I mind if his boss, Eric, sat in on the meeting and monitored his performance? Would that be all right by me? I told him it would.

Over the course of the next 55 minutes, Tom went through his pitch in great and stultifying detail. Like most salespeople, I'm usually very easy to sell to. Still, Tom wasn't to know this and he went through his pitch with studied professionalism. Following the classic AIDA acronym, Tom made me AWARE of the benefits of the product (Keeps out not just the cold, but also burglars). He created an INCENTIVE (10 per cent off) and then tried to stimulate DESIRE. It was this bit that needed some work. I recall that the unique selling point was that his windows were made out of "cold rolled steel". I don't know why that's better than any other kind, but Tom had a very languid way of saying "cold rolled steel" which really brought out the assonance, and he kept saying it again and again, so it was evidently a good thing, but I was no clearer why it should be any better than, say, hot rolled steel or cold steel that hadn't been rolled.

A good salesman, they say, knows his product, but I wasn't convinced. I needed time to think about it, I said. No I didn't, said Tom, he'd just go over it again so that I understood. The only thing I understood was that Tom wasn't going to leave until I'd bought his windows.

On and on he went, clearly sensing that there was a deal to be closed here. He went over the Awareness again (quoting crime figures and wind speeds), reiterated the incentive (10 per cent off) and banged on about the cold rolled bleeding steel. He even asked the textbook sort of open questions: "If we could get the right price, would you sign up tonight?"

I cold-rolled my eyes and looked at the time. He'd been there for almost an hour and a half.

Finally he went for the call to ACTION. If I was to sign tonight, he'd knock not 10 per cent but 20 per cent off and my bay window would cost only £1,750.

"That seems a bit pricey," I said. Tom had got his pen out.

"No problem, we can work out a finance package. You can pay by instalments."

"That doesn't make it any cheaper, though, does it?" I replied.

"It makes it more affordable." Tom smiled and, edging forward, offered me the pen and order form.

"Have you got any windows in wood?" I asked.

"No, all our windows are UPVC," said Tom, highlighting the two spaces I needed to sign. "They are guaranteed for a lifetime. You'll never have to change them again."

I think he may have been licking his lips.

"The thing is, this is a conservation area, so we're not allowed to put UPVC windows in. Only wooden ones. Sorry."

Tom looked like a man who'd discovered his wife in bed with his best friend. I spoke gently to Eric.

"Perhaps you should mention that in future, it might save some time. Still, thanks for your time, you should do well with that cold rolled steel thing."

A few days later, when I got a quote for £400 including fitting, I realised that I had been a local council environmental committee meeting away from wasting £1,350.

Companies make outrageous claims for the benefits of product X, which is absolutely no different to product Y, because they know we are stupid and that we will believe them. Take soap powder, for example. I expect you probably demonstrate some kind of brand loyalty in this area. Are you a Fairy Family, a Persil Household or an Ariel Couple? I wonder. Are you a powder or liquid user? I also assume you can explain your purchasing decision. Is your powder cheaper? Does it wash whiter than white? Maybe it's kind to colours. Now here's three points to consider:

1  Are your clothes actually any cleaner than your friends' and colleagues'?

2 Do you know what washing powder they use?
3 Can you tell what washing powder people use just by looking at their clean clothes?

Thought not.

We celebrate our ignorance every day through the items we place in our shopping baskets, the food we eat, the newspapers, books and magazines we read, the TV programmes and films we watch, and the music we listen to. Ten-year-old me with his faith in science would be horrified not at just how unscientific we've become, but at how complacent we are about it.

"So what?" you might be saying. "What has science ever given us?"

The answer is everything. And the fact you know so little about it means you've almost certainly wasted a considerable amount of your hard-earned money on things you don't need.

Here is a short test I've devised to assess your own level of scientific expertise. We'll explore the answers in the following chapters.

1 How does electricity work?
2 $0.20 \times \frac{1}{4}(4.25 - 1\frac{1}{2}) = ?$
3 How much fat is in "low-fat" food? Less than:

    20 per cent
    10 per cent
    5 per cent
    3 per cent
    1 per cent

4  Homoeopathy: true or false? (NB: Before considering the answer, you may refer to these wise words – "Many of today's complementary therapies are rooted in ancient traditions that intuitively understood the need to maintain balance and harmony with our minds, bodies and the natural world.")

5  How old is Planet Earth?

6  What are the seven signs of ageing?

7  How would you get rid of "soap scum, lime-scale, ground-in dirt and tough grime"?

8  How do we get drinkable water?

Tie-breaker: Should Britain scrap the pound and embrace the euro?

# 6 | **How Does Electricity Work?**

Electricity is not as new as you might think. It's actually been around for a very long time, but it's only in the last 150 years that we've worked out something useful to do with it. The Ancient Greeks were aware of static electricity. Pythagoras (he of the theorem) may not have discovered it, but he did write a lot about static electricity, which he created by rubbing two pieces of amber together. Interestingly, the Greek word for amber is *Elektron*.

Static wasn't much use for anything other than making your hair stand on end or giving people electric shocks when you shook hands, so the history of electricity is rather moribund for the next 2,000 years, right up until 1752, when American writer, publisher, scientist and diplomat Benjamin Franklin proved that lightning and the spark from amber were one and the same thing. He did this by fastening an iron spike to the string of a silken kite, which he then flew during a thunderstorm. When lightning flashed, a tiny spark jumped from the spike to his wrist.

Electricity is caused by the movement of electrons, tiny negatively charged particles that surround every atom. The electrons can be made to flow from atom to atom in metals, and as long as the wires are connected in a circuit, electricity can flow easily. Electricity is produced at a power station. Fuel is used to boil water; when the water boils, the high-pressure steam produced is used to drive turbines, which in turn generate electricity. These "generators" are nothing more than enormous magnets that spin inside coils of metal wire. Electricity and magnetism are related physical forces, and it's the movement of the magnets which causes electricity to flow in the wires.

The flow of these electrons is called electric current, and this current likes to travel back to where it came from, in kind of a circle, which is called a "circuit". So the power lines that extend out from a power station and into our homes and offices all eventually lead all the way back to the power station.

The volume of electricity flowing through power lines is much greater than any of us need, so transformers are used to distribute energy to each household. Transformers drain off a percentage of the energy carried in the power line and transmit it to smaller circuits, like those in an office or house.

In each building there are a number of circuits, each allowing for different amounts of power. Finally, when you plug in an appliance, the electricity can be used to create light or heat or even sound. It can even run motors that will keep things cold.

If you got this answer I'm guessing you're probably either a teacher or have an educational background in science – either way, well done. If you didn't get it, don't worry – most people have no idea how any of the basic utilities work. Not even the people selling them.

On what seems like a daily basis, I get calls at home and at work from people asking me whether, first, I'm happy with my electricity supply (that old open question again) and, second, whether I'd like to see if they can supply it more cheaply.

"Well, the stuff we've got now seems to work pretty

well," I respond. "It's compatible with all the office equipment. And to be honest, I'm very happy with the level of service from our current supplier: it's always there whenever we want it and it's fast. Pretty much every time we turn on the switch there it is. We certainly never seem to run out of it."

I'm also always interested to know – exactly – how they are able to supply me with cheaper electricity. Is there a quality issue: are they trying to sell me something lower grade than the stuff I'm getting at the moment? Electrical cava rather than champagne, so to speak.

And how will this inferior supply affect the performance of my computer equipment?

Will I still be able to run Windows XP? Perhaps, hidden in the small print, there are restrictions about what I can use my new electricity for: heat and light, yes, but I'm afraid our stuff is no good for keeping things cold or listening to music.

Perhaps they're using unethical supply methods: is my electricity being put together by ten-year-old orphans in an Indonesian sweatshop? And how much is it going to cost to take the old supply out and put the new stuff in …?

At this point they usually either hang up or ask me whether I'm happy with my gas supply.

# 7 | $0.20 \times \frac{1}{4}(4.25 - 1\frac{1}{2}) =$

Answer: 0.138.

Have you ever wondered why it is considered socially acceptable to say, "I'm no good at maths"? You wouldn't, for example, hear anyone proudly extol the fact that they can't read, would you? Yet people often announce they are no good at maths in a manner that suggests they are actually rather proud of it.

There is an argument that numeracy is less important in everyday life than literacy. As long as we can count, we can get by. We can tell the time, work out whether we need to speed up or slow down in the car, and the supermarket checkout will sort our change out for us. For many people only basic numeracy skills are necessary (and basic numeracy skills are easier to pick up than basic literacy skills).

Indeed, the penalties for the illiterate seem to far outweigh those for being innumerate. You wouldn't be able to read a newspaper, fill out a form, order from a menu, or follow road signs or written instructions. You wouldn't even be able to operate your iPod. Most jobs, aside from basic manual work, would be closed to you.

So you might be forgiven for thinking that being bad at maths doesn't really matter, but in reality, being numerate has a profound impact on how successful you are, far, far greater, in fact, than being literate.

According to the University of Life Long Learning,

> Both literacy and numeracy have a profound
> effect on earnings. However, numeracy seems

> to have a more powerful effect than literacy.
> Low earnings are much more likely if one has
> poor basic skills than if one has good basic
> skills, but the difference in earnings is greater
> for numeracy than for literacy.
>
> At the national level, numeracy has a
> profound effect on the average productivity of
> the workforce and explains a significant
> proportion of the difference in economic
> performance between nations.

People use being bad at maths to excuse all kinds of incompetence. Perfectly good businesses go bust because the MD couldn't get his "head around the figures".

Matt and Luke Goss, stars of slightly unnerving 1980s teenybop band Bros, lost an entire fortune because they didn't understand the difference between gross profit (the amount of money you receive in a single year) and net profit (the amount of money you have left once you have deducted all your costs).

It's not really a difficult concept to grasp, though, is it?

Like Bros, Robert Maxwell, the evil newspaper magnate and kleptomaniac, failed to understand the importance of profit, preferring instead to plunder staff pension schemes to prop up his ailing business empire.

Continuing this theme of corporate greed, Enron, the American energy company, went spectacularly bust in 2001, owing over $17 billion. Financial incompetence and greed were the main contributing factors, underlined by this bizarre admission from disgraced CFO Andrew Farstow, during cross-examination at the fraud trial in March 2006:

> I believe I was extremely greedy, I lost my
> moral compass* and I have done terrible
> things that I very much regret …
> I believed I was being [a hero] within the
> culture of corruption that Enron had, the
> culture that rewarded financial reporting as
> opposed to rewarding economic value.

That's all right, then. I suppose the lesson here is slightly more complicated than the one learned by Matt and Luke: that publishing high-quality annual reports, on 180gsm paper, filled with lies, is no substitute for making a profit (either net or gross in this instance).

A final example from the UK: Marconi, the defence-turned-telecoms business, managed to turn a £2.5 billion cash pile into £4.3 billion of debt in just five years. It did this by selling a lot of really good businesses that made things – such as Hotpoint – and using the money to pay massively over the odds for rubbish US telecom companies at the height of the tech boom. Still, at least this story has a happy ending. Although the company nearly folded, one of the captains of its demise, John Mayo, was emptied out with a £600,000 thank-you for all his hard work.

As Leo Bloom, the mild-mannered accountant in the

---

* I'd love a moral compass. I wonder whether it points to magnetic greed?

1968 film *The Producers* said, you can sell only 100 per cent of anything. Percentages cause plenty of problems. Footballers perennially struggle with the concept. Giving 100 per cent just isn't enough.

In March 2005 England captain David Beckham guaranteed that the team would be giving 110 per cent in the match against Azerbaijan. This might be enough for somnambulant Sven-Göran Eriksson, but the previous incumbent, Kevin Keegan, often demanded 1,000 percent when he was manager of Newcastle.

Even in the business world, where you'd expect figures to be given more respect, percentages still cause a bit of bother. In the popular TV series *The Apprentice*, one of the candidates offered to give Sir Alan Sugar 150 per cent. Sir Alan wasn't impressed, but then he did use to run a football club.

The percentage figure most of us struggle with is the annual percentage rate or APR. The APR is the cost of credit consumers pay expressed as a simple percentage. You will see it quoted on credit card and loan applications, and it allows you to calculate the amount of money you will pay. And the higher the APR, the more expensive the credit.

For example, if you borrow £100 over one year at an APR of 20 per cent you will have to pay the lender back an additional £20, making you liable for a total of £120 or:

$$100 + (100/100 \times 20) = 120$$

Simple, really, except that an Institute of Financial Services survey in June 2004 estimated that eight out of ten people

$$0.20 \times \frac{1}{4}(4.25 - 1\frac{1}{2}) =$$

don't actually know what APR means. A sizeable minority of those surveyed thought it was short for April.

And this fact becomes even scarier when you consider the record levels of personal debt in the UK. Britain's personal debt is increasing at a rate of £1 million every four minutes.*

The number of people declaring themselves bankrupt is also at record levels. Personal borrowing in the UK stands at more than £1 trillion, and this, coupled with the recent rises in interest rates, has led to a growing number of individual insolvencies. Department of Trade and Industry figures for January–March 2005 showed bankruptcies up 28 per cent on the same period in 2004, to 13,229.

Perhaps we all need to work a little bit harder at our sums. And while we're on the subject of percentages …

---

* Rupert Jones, "Britons rack up £1m debt every four minutes", *Guardian*, 3 June 2004.

# 8 | **How Much Fat Is in "Low-Fat" Food?**

To qualify as "low-fat", food must have a fat content of less than 3 per cent.

Britain has the unenviable accolade of having the highest rates of obesity in western Europe. And we are getting fatter. According to a report by the Consumers' Association, "In England, obesity has tripled since 1980, and nearly one third of children aged two to 15 are now classed as overweight or obese."*

Ironically, we also have a well-earned reputation for having the worst food in Europe. We eat like pigs; so consequently we look like pigs as well.

Travel abroad and you'll struggle to find a traditional British restaurant ... actually, that's a bit disingenuous of me, isn't it? Travel abroad to a holiday destination popular with the Brits like the Costa del Sol or the Canary Islands and you'll find the place crawling with traditional British restaurants providing traditional British dishes like fish and chips, pie and chips, roast beef and chicken tikka masala. Let's face it: British food is the pits.

"But Steve, what about Gordon, Jamie and Delia?" I hear you cry. "What about Gary Rhodes, Nigella and Antony Worrall Thompson, who wrote a book about weight loss after seeing himself on *I'm a Celebrity Get Me Out of Here*?"

OK, at its very best, at its Michelin starred finest, in book-endorsed restaurants, I'll grant you, British food competes with the best in Europe. I'm assuming, however,

---

* "The facts behind fast food", Consumers' Association, July 2005.

that you're not on first-name terms with the maître d' at the Ivy and that the closest you've ever come to reserving a table at a celebrity-endorsed restaurant is that time you went to that place that was featured on Ramsay's *Kitchen Nightmares*. For a laugh!

But the stuff that normal people buy and eat on a daily basis is a different bag of offal altogether. Those same chefs are always at pains to point out how much easier it is to buy high-quality pancetta from a corner shop in a down-at-heel suburb of Naples than it is where you live. That is if you've got a corner shop left at all.

The UK's national dish is now officially chicken tikka masala. Interestingly, no one really knows what chicken tikka masala actually is. There is no recipe as such, but one thing's for sure, it's about as Indian as Peter Sellers. Our national dish was born in the 1960s and owes its origins to a restaurant in Glasgow. A diner asked for some gravy to go with his chicken tikka, so the bemused chef added some spices to a tin of Campbell's tomato soup and chicken tikka masala was born.

I believe chicken tikka masala's position at the top of the British culinary tree will be somewhat short lived. I am predicting confidently that within the next three years it will be replaced by a dish with an even less prestigious pedigree, one that will really show just how far our culinary history has come. I'm talking about a modern dish that is easy to prepare, and is even outstripping takeaway food in terms of sales. A dish that's so popular it is now all that some of us eat. I am talking, of course, about the Ready Meal.

Was it because our food was so bad to begin with that

we fell for the ready meal? Or was it, I wonder, because of our desire to look towards America, the only country in the world that's fatter than us, rather than to Europe as our primary cultural influence? Or was it in fact due to the domination (decimation?) of our high streets by the super-markets, which generate much bigger margins from processed foods than from fresh ingredients?

Maybe it's a combination of the three, and a few more I haven't thought of, but whatever the reason, we are now eating more processed food than ever before. And unless you're a supermarket shareholder, this is empirically not a good thing.

Ready meals mark a cultural nadir: the antithesis of healthy eating, they look awful, smell awful, taste awful and, by golly, they're awful for you as well. A report from the Consumers' Association suggested that ready meals might be *even more unhealthy* than takeaway meals. I've been looking forward to writing the next sentence since I started this chap-ter. That means takeaways are actually a healthier alternative to ready meals. Crikey – it's not often you get to say that about takeaway food. Previously you could have legally writ-ten that sentence only if you'd been talking about rat poison, lard or sweets bought from the tuck shop at Chernobyl.

Looking at food labels should be the easiest way of identifying whether or not the food contained within con-tains too much fat or not. Unfortunately, as I pointed out earlier, we're all thickos. And this is something the people who sell processed food to us know only too well. They know that with a little help from their silver-tongued advertising agencies, we'll soon be as confused as ten-year-old me was when he was introduced to his dazzlingly beautiful new student teacher, Miss Rae.

Legally, if a food claims it is "fat free" it must have less than 0.15g fat per 100g. Likewise, "low-fat" food must contain less than 3g fat per 100g. It's also worth remembering that any more than 20g fat per 100g is, generally speaking, a hell of a lot.

Now that's nice and straightforward, but here's where the "Miss Rae effect" comes into play. Manufacturers know that there are rules for "fat free" and "low-fat", so cunningly, like that great musician Peter Andre, they just make up their own terms. The results are insania.

"Reduced fat" doesn't mean anything beyond the fact that the food in question must contain 25 per cent less fat than the equivalent standard product. So it's healthier in the way that a takeaway is healthier than a ready meal, i.e. not at all, really.

There is no legal definition of the word "lite". Actually, I'm not sure that there is a dictionary definition. My own research, however, appears to reveal that this term actually means "A product that appears to be either healthier or containing fewer calories than an alternative, but which in fact isn't and doesn't."

Here are some more terms that you'll find on ready meals which have absolutely no meaning whatsoever. They may make you think your shopping basket is brimming with healthy goodness. It isn't.

- Lean
- Natural

- Original recipe
- Country fresh
- Farm
- Home-baked
- Lighter
- Traditional
- Special
- Original
- Selected
- Wholesome
- Fresh
- Healthy
- Gourmet
- Finest

Wholesome items can often be found to contain distinctly unwholesome-sounding ingredients such as guar gum, antioxidants, additives, e-numbers and preservatives. Think about it, though – what would something that was truly "farm fresh" actually be like? Milk that is still at cow's udder temperature? Legs of lamb, still twitching, before rigor mortis has set in? And those veal steaks: so fresh you can still taste the fear.

It's worse than this, though. The manufacturers are not content with trying to convince us that the stuff in these brightly packaged, ready-for-the-microwave plastic trays offer us a healthy lifestyle choice. They stare us right in the eye and, without blinking, maintain that what we are about to eat will be all but indistinguishable from the kind of meal we'd get in a Michelin-starred restaurant.

You do really have to admire their balls here. What kind of idiot would think that this gloop in a box, produced and packaged on an industrial estate in Dundee by a bunch of acne-scarred adolescents, could compare with a gourmet meal prepared in one of the UK's finest restaurants? I'm not Derren Brown but sales figures don't lie. The odds are that you've got a chilled meal in the fridge.

Like all "good ideas", ready meals offer their producers much greater potential than solving the original problem. Imagine the meeting:

> *Senior manager*: "Brilliant work, fellers. Sales are going through the roof. We really have managed to convince people that this shit is restaurant quality. Maybe I'm eating in the wrong restaurants."
> *Marketing lackey*: "Or the right ones, sir!"
> *All*: (Laugh)
> *Product guy*: "Hey, maybe there's something in that. If people really do believe this stuff is like the kind of food you get in a restaurant, why don't we open a restaurant that sells ready meals?"
> *Marketing lackey*: "We could give it a faux Euro-sounding name and position it as a gourmet-style outlet and really increase our margin. We'd be saving a fortune on back-room staff. All the meals could be prepared centrally, chilled and then delivered to the site to be reheated. It's genius. We'll make a fortune."
> *All*: (Laugh)

> *Senior manager*: "I love it. Let's do lunch. Pot
> Noodle, anyone?"

This is happening now. In restaurant chains with generic menus the main elements of a dish are being prepared centrally, chilled and then distributed to the individual restaurants, where they are reheated on-site once they have been ordered. Surely this is a ready meal in any other name? Let me clarify things by relating the following real-life experience.

Recently, on the way back from a day in the park, my wife and I took the kids to Café Rouge for lunch. I'm not proud, we were hungry, and having developed fiercely middle-class sensibilities about fast food, since we read *Fast Food Nation* and saw *Supersize Me*, there's no way we are going to expose our little smashers to the corporate evil of McDonald's. No way. Except on birthdays. And special occasions.

For those of you who don't know it, Café Rouge is a chain of restaurants that offers, in its own words, "A combination of delicious food, great wines and a real ambience. Café Rouge has embodied the style and *je ne sais quoi* of European dining since it opened back in 1989."

Sounds great, doesn't it? And if nothing else, *la famille* McKevitt is always up for a bit of *je ne sais quoi*.

Sadly, the reality fell somewhat short of this mission statement. Café Rouge is a faux-French restaurant serving faux-bistro-style food that is priced attractively for the shareholder. For an authentic version of this facsimile, I'd imagine you'd have to go to a very specific part of France – EuroDisney.

This isn't a book about fast food and, with my deadline looming, I haven't had time to go undercover and find out *exactly* how Café Rouge prepares its delicious meals, so I'll relate my own experience and let you draw your own conclusions.

We placed our order with a waiter appropriately attired in a classic white apron. Fiona plumped for a French stalwart, *moules et frites*. The kids, typically less adventurous, went for the pancakes. *Bientôt*, our waiter returned. *Malheureusement*, there was a problem with the order.

"I'm sorry," he said, "we've run out of chips. Would Madam like boiled potatoes with her mussels instead?"

I laughed. I thought he was joking. He wasn't. I told him I thought I could see a way out of this and pointed out that, rather than boiling the potatoes, couldn't they cut them into smaller pieces and drop them into a pan of boiling oil? He looked puzzled; rather than reply, he decided to explain that that wasn't the only problem.

"We've also run out of pancakes. Would the children like to choose something else?"

Ingredients for pancakes: flour, eggs, milk. I never like causing a fuss in restaurants (it's not a British thing, it's just I don't want somebody spitting – or worse – in my food), but I made an exception here. At the risk of sounding like Michael Winner, I said I found it incredible that a bistro that prided itself on the fact that it "embodied the style and *je ne sais quoi* of European dining since it opened back in 1989" should be struggling to rustle up a plate of chips and a couple of pancakes, for only £27.50.

It was then that the waiter said something incredible: "I'll have a word with Chef."

"Chef"? "Have a word"? This place has a *chef*? I tried to imagine how a conversation with a Chef like that would unfold.

"Complaint from table thirteen, Chef. They say the *steak au poivre* is cold."

Chef, who in real life is a media studies student called Colin, is puzzled; he picks a packet out of the bin and scratches his head.

"I can't think why. It says microwave on full power for five minutes; which is exactly what I did. I followed the recipe to the letter."

Of course, I might be wrong. Perhaps Café Rouge prepares all its meals from fresh ingredients on-site and in this isolated case Chef had simply mislaid the recipe for chips. And the one for pancakes.

Needless to say, we declined the offer of whatever's French for boiled potatoes – not sure they have them over there – and went next door to McDonald's for a couple of Happy Meals.

"Is this a special occasion?" asked the kids.

The idea is that tucking into a reheated meal is as good as it gets. And this message appears to be getting through to people. Here are three quotes from delighted customers taken from Tesco's own website:

> Heather loved Pork with a Cream and Cider Sauce (£2.89).
>
> "It looked lovely in its box, with broccoli pieces and apple chunks on top, apparently

Granny Smiths. I couldn't believe it was a ready meal but it microwaved in five minutes and tasted as good as it looked. When are the desserts coming out?"

Darren tried Beef in Chianti with Roasted Potatoes and Vegetables (£2.89).

"I liked the idea of a 'healthy' red wine sauce and it sounded dead posh. The beef was tender, my veggie portions, broccoli and carrots, were in there too and it filled me up."

Ryan and Shane both went for Chicken Tikka with Fragrant Rice and Raita Dressing (£2.49).

"Chicken tikka's our favourite curry, and I can usually eat more than Shane. This one looked very healthy – there were red peppers and spinach – though it wasn't as thick as the usual take-away Dad normally gets. But we were still full up."*

Mm-hmm. Who needs restaurants or home cooking? Pass me that plastic tray and let the feast begin.

Are ready meals useless? Probably not if you're either a manufacturer or a grocer, who is looking to maximise profits by adding value to a set of raw materials, but almost certainly yes if you're anyone else. But there is one

---

* "Welcome to the new food revolution", *Today at Tesco*, Tesco.com, 2 February 2006.

final point to make against these cartons of chilled filth, and it concerns not their consumption but their disposal.

People – and especially middle-class people – are becoming more aware about the health implications of living exclusively on a diet of fast food. In the UK the better-off households produce an average of 5kg more waste per week than working-class households, and people who live in cities, surrounded by convenience and amenity, are much more wasteful than those who live in the country, for whom even a trip to the local shop for a pint of milk requires forward planning. The biggest culprits of all are single, middle-class city-dwellers – Britain's fastest growing socio-economic group – who, surprise, surprise, also happen to be the biggest consumers of ready meals.

A century ago, 80 per cent of household waste was made up of dust and ash. In 2006 packaging accounts for 35 per cent of the weight and 50 per cent of the volume of household waste.

Professor Bill Rathje, from the University of Arizona, is an expert in household refuse. He has highlighted a trend among young urban professionals which he calls "the fast lane syndrome". This group is not only consuming ready meals, but is also buying fresh ingredients and produce, in the vain hope that they will make the time to cook it. They kid themselves that ready meals form no more than a stand-by, but studies show that it is the ready meals which get eaten and the fresh meat and vegetables which get thrown away. We produce over 100 million tonnes of rubbish every year in the UK and household waste is currently increasing at a rate of 3 per cent a year.

Despite the "fact" that "Many of today's complementary therapies are rooted in ancient traditions that intuitively understood the need to maintain balance and harmony with our minds, bodies and the natural world" the answer is, absolutely and categorically, 100 per cent false.

The quote comes from that notable medical authority, Prince Charles, during an impassioned speech to the World Health Assembly in Geneva, in which he outlined his philosophy of holistic care to an enthralled audience of the world's health ministers. He urged every country to develop a plan for integrating conventional and alternative medicine.*

This was the same Prince Charles who, in 1982, upon being elected president of the BMA, lectured doctors on the benefits of healing. Naturally, expecting some hostility to what any normal person would view as compelling evidence for his sectioning under the Mental Health Act, the Prince used his reading of Albert Camus to prepare the basis of his defence: "Perhaps, we just have to accept it is God's will that the unorthodox individual is doomed to years of frustration, ridicule and failure in order to act out his role in the scheme of things, until his day arrives and mankind is ready to receive his message."

I'm not one of those people who believes that the Prince of Wales should stick to subjects he knows something about – you may as well sew his mouth up with darning

* Reuters, 23 May 2006.

wool if that were the case – and were it not for the fact that the government actually agrees with him I'd happily notch up a fresh reason why I take no notice of the royal family. I firmly believe that if I ignore them they might go away.*

In his fantastic polemic aimed at reclaiming the rational thought of the Enlightenment, *How Mumbo-Jumbo Conquered the World*, Francis Wheen describes how a feng shui consultant, Renuka Wickramaratne, was hired by the government to advise on how we could improve the inner cities: "Red and orange flowers would reduce crime and introducing a water feature would reduce poverty. I was brought up with this ancient knowledge."

Town planners take heed: there is much wisdom here.

Western medicine comes in for a great deal of criticism. The state of the health service – always, it would seem, in crisis – is a salient issue for everyone, and the newspapers are regularly filled with stories about people who got the wrong treatment/the right treatment but too late/no treatment at all. Waiting lists for having a bunion removed can be up to 1,000 years long (depending upon which part of the country you live in) or about twelve minutes if you're willing to go private. If you do get treated it's normally by an unqualified junior doctor from the subcontinent or eastern Europe who's been working for 148 hours without

---

* Prince Charles appears to be aware of this fact, and is doing his darnedest to make sure I fail. I once caught a documentary while staying at my mum's house some years ago, in which the Prince of Wales was playing football with the young Princes Harry and William. Nothing wrong with that except that, first, he played the game like lots of posh people who've been to public school do – i.e. like a girl – and second, he was wearing a kilt and sporran at the time. Burned. Into. My. Memory.

food, drink or sleep and whose communication skills are on a par with Helen Keller's. And even if you are lucky to make a recovery, the chances are you'll be infected by the deadly flesh-eating MRA virus. You'd be mad to go into a hospital! Mad, I tell you! At least, that's what it said in the *Daily Mail*.

The health service could be better, and I've got one or two radical ideas of my own for improving it, which I'll share with you in a moment, but first let's look at a few facts.

Despite all the criticism and evidence to the contrary, we are living in a golden age, in terms of public health. Life expectancy is at an all-time high, in stark contrast to infant mortality, which is at an all-time low. There's a very good chance you'll live to be fit and well into your eighties. Your children might live to be older than 100.

Many of the diseases that decimated the population up to our grandparents' generation have, in the UK at least, been largely confined to medical textbooks. Cases of diphtheria, typhoid, syphilis, smallpox and polio are very rare or unheard of. Childhood diseases like measles, mumps and whooping cough no longer affect our children in significant numbers.

Even where there isn't necessarily a cure, patients suffering from many kinds of cancer, Aids and hepatitis can look forward to a much longer life expectancy thanks to innovative treatments born out of years of painstaking research. Looking forward, there is much confidence that stem cell research will offer similar benefits to sufferers of genetically inherited diseases.

I could go on, but the point is that the standard of medical care available today, compared to, say, any other point in history, is phenomenally good. Yes, of course it could be better, and of course the health service could be better run, but that is an issue for the government and shouldn't undermine the intrinsic quality of care and the work of the health professionals who provide it, and the weight of scientific research that has been built up over hundreds of years, which lies at its basis.

And now for my revolutionary idea. What I'm proposing is that anybody who has sought treatment from homoeopathic, complementary or New Age medicine should immediately be considered, by this action, to have excluded themselves from free treatment on the NHS.*

In scientific trials, homoeopathy has time and again been clinically proven to have no greater effect than a placebo. That homoeopathy is bunk is a view shared by pretty much all the scientific community. So how come it's more popular now than ever?

The English poet and essayist G. K. Chesterton is reported to have said, "When people stop believing in God, they don't believe in nothing – they believe in anything." There is a theory that our belief in a deity developed as we evolved the ability to identify cause and effect: an ability that makes us unique in the animal kingdom.†

---

* I was originally thinking of extending this to include "Anyone who has ever participated in a Five Live phone-in", but on reflection feel this may be a little harsh.

† Although admittedly this is only one ability of many. Man is the only animal to use language/make complex tools/kill for sport/play badminton, etc.

We learned that if it rains there will be more water in the waterhole and that animals will come to drink. We learned that if we sharpen a stone and tie it to a stick we have a weapon we could throw at the animals when they came to drink, thus allowing us to kill and eat them. And then we learned that the meal would taste better if we cooked it over the fire. And then we learned how to make barbecue sauce.

Clearly much of this arcane knowledge has been lost to the people who work in my local Café Rouge, but a by-product of the development of this skill is that, as a species, we are constantly looking for meaning. When faced with an effect without an obvious cause, the branch of a tree falling down in the forest or a flash of lightning, for example, we'd fill in the gaps as best we could: the work of spirits, fairies or gods.

Homoeopathy, like ready meals or the TV phenomenon that is *Most Haunted*,* is merely a modern symptom of our innate gullibility. It's not just the admen who are exploiting us; the quacks are getting in on the act as well.

Homoeopathy was founded at the turn of the nineteenth century by a German physician, Samuel Hahnemann. His guiding principles remain the bedrock of homoeopathic medicine today. That's right, homoeopathy takes absolutely no notice of *any* scientific or medical discoveries that have been made over the past 200 years –

---

* Surely this is as blatant a case for prosecution under the Trades Description Act as there's ever been. *Least Haunted* would be much closer to the mark.

like, say, the discovery of bacteria, viruses or antibiotics. But don't let me put you off.

The main principle of homoeopathy is the so-called Law of Similars. In essence this is very close to the basic idea of vaccination: if you're given a little of what's bad for you, then that will stimulate the body to fight back. The difference is that homoeopathic remedies reverse the mainstream medical principle that the strength of the drug increases with the dose. The other main principle of homoeopathy, the Law of Infinitesimals, states that the cure's effectiveness decreases with the dose. So the less you take, the better the cure.

The mathematics involved in homoeopathy are astounding. Remedies are often so diluted that the chances of them containing even one molecule of the healing agent are thousands to one. The reason why its performance is no better than that of a placebo is quite simply because that's what it is.

## 10 | **How Old Is Planet Earth?**

Answer: 4.55 billion years old (+ or – 1 per cent).

An enormous amount of time and effort went into determining the age of the earth. The actual age of our planet has occupied scholars for centuries. In 1701 an Irish bishop called James Usher announced that the world was created on the late afternoon of Sunday, 23 October, in the year 4004 BC.

The real answer was only discovered 250 years later by a geophysicist called Clair Patterson. In 1953, he made this discovery by assuming correctly that meteorites were formed at around the same time as the earth, and since they didn't come from the earth, they couldn't have been contaminated by it. He measured their age using a radioactive lead dating technique, and Bob's your uncle. Obviously it was much more complicated than this in practice, but he successfully put an end to over two hundred years of scientific debate.

There have been countless polls which show that over 42 per cent of Americans believe the world is less than 10,000 years old. Why do they believe this? Because it says so in the Bible. Which explains why, if you go online now, you'll find literally thousands of websites disputing Patterson's figure. These websites have two things in common. First, they are all run by Creationists and, second, they are all wrong. Which only goes to show – to paraphrase Chesterton – that if you believe in God, you'll believe in nothing.

I'm not interested in Creationists. What I am interested

in is helping you to understand what an awfully long time 4.55 billion years is.

About 500 million years ago, a fish crawled out of the ocean in what is now know as the Cambrian period and decided to give this living on land lark a bit of a go. From that bold fish, all birds, reptiles and mammals evolved. I appreciate you might be a bit sceptical, so here's a brief exercise to show you just how long 500 million years is.

I want you to count up to 500 million steadily. (It's going to take a bit of time, so we'll let you have eight hours' sleep each night.)

Start now: 1 ... 2 ... 3 ... 4... 5 ...
... 499,999,998 ... 499,999,999 ... 500,000,000.

Well done. Now consider that this exercise took us only the best part of 24 years. And that's just to count to 500 million. Believe me (and every scientist in the world), that's plenty of time for life's splendour to evolve.

If you didn't know this already, I hope you find it interesting. And that's the point really – I find the whole notion of evolution over this period of time awe inspiring, fascinating and uplifting, yet most people aren't interested at all. They'd prefer to believe lies or exist in blissful ignorance.

I recently took my daughter to see the movie *Ice Age 2*. One of my friends was outraged at the concept of the movie: how could there be an *Ice Age 2*, when there was, after all, only one Ice Age? Alas for him, but great news for movie franchisers, there have actually been over a thousand ice ages.

Science is fascinating, far more fascinating than, say, Jade Goody, but in terms of media cachet, it just can't seem to compete. What we know about the world around us is amazing: we deserve to be amazed by it. Why should we have to rely on pretending there are ghosties communicating to us through a Scouse medium and a former *Blue Peter* presenter for entertainment? Or be patronised into thinking we might be intrigued to find out what "the actress" Sadie Frost did next?*

When it's done well – *Planet Earth* on BBC1, for example – science attracts and captivates millions of viewers. Unfortunately programmes of this calibre are infrequent, and usually appear only when the renewal of the BBC's broadcast licence is up for review. If it's on TV at all, science is either done badly – *You're Greedy So You're Fat*, presented by Gillian McQuack with her diploma in bollox from the University of Some Bloke's Attic in California, for a completely fictional example – or is of the harum-scarum, run-for-the-hills variety of *Horizon* and *Equinox*.

In fact most of the science on TV takes place in between the programmes themselves.

The only problem is, it isn't very scientific.

---

* Disappear from our screens for ever with any luck.

## 11 | **What Are the Seven Signs of Ageing?**

Answer: It depends on who you ask.

According to the customer service department at Procter & Gamble, the makers of Oil of Olay, the seven signs of ageing are:

1  Lines and wrinkles
2  Rough skin texture
3  Dullness of skin's appearance
4  Larger appearance of pores
5  Blotchiness
6  Dry skin
7  Age spots.

And not:*

1  Cerebral atrophy
2  Hypermetropia (long-sightedness)
3  Presbyacusis (deafness)
4  Osteoarthritis
5  Hypertension (high blood pressure)
6  Increased risk of myocardial infarction (heart attack) and stroke
7  Increased risk of falling and fractures.

---

* According to the *Oxford Textbook of Medicine*.

And definitely not:*

1  Voting Conservative
2  Forgetting where you've put your keys
3  Reading the *Daily Express*
4  Listening to Radio 4
5  Buying shoes because they look comfy
6  Not knowing which song is number one in the "Hit Parade"
7  Weighing 2 stone more than you used to.

I make that 21 signs of ageing in all, but only seven of these signs could be found in the *Oxford Textbook of Medicine*. You might be interested to note that Oil of Olay is equally effective at treating all 21 signs of ageing. Which is to say it isn't.

I bet you're stunned, aren't you? Has Citizen McKevitt just taken on The Man in the shape of Procter & Gamble, by effectively rubbishing the claims it makes for one of its flagship products, Oil of Olay? Fair play to him and his brave publisher, but they'll get surely eaten alive.

Sadly nothing could be farther from the truth.

Cosmetics companies choose their words with incredible care. Procter & Gamble has never claimed that Oil of Olay could "treat" *the* seven signs of ageing; it claims only that it can "fight" seven signs of ageing, which is a very different thing altogether. I could, for example, say I was going

---

* According to Steve McKevitt, BA (Hons).

to "fight" Mike Tyson, but it's just highly unlikely that I will "beat" him.

Oil of Olay is a decent, if somewhat overpriced, skin moisturiser and everyone agrees that keeping your skin moisturised is a good thing. But the elixir of eternal youth in a jar it ain't.

Cosmetics companies are brilliant at selling us things we don't need. Their marketing and advertising are packed with just enough information to persuade us that product X is good for us. They don't lie – far from it, they only tell the truth. They just don't tell all of it.

Olay's latest brand extension is a product called Regenerist, which contains an amino-peptide which, P & G claims, is crucial for collagen formation. This is perfectly true. But there are around twenty amino acids altogether which are crucial for collagen formation, and we normally get these from our food, not from a poultice we daub on our faces.

Still, you can't fault this approach in terms of delivering results. In the UK in 2002, £652 million was spent by a credulous public on anti-ageing products and 72,000 cosmetic surgery procedures were carried out.*

Anti-ageing products are big business, but the reality is that there is no miracle ingredient that is going to make you look ten years younger. In fact the most effective agents are nothing more than the now dreadfully unfashionable and boring vitamins A, C and E.

---

* Claire Roberts, *Anti Ageing Products: The Bare Facts*.

The most important factors in looking young for your age are all to do with lifestyle. Around 30 per cent of facial ageing is genetic, but the remaining 70 per cent is down to repetitive sunlight, smoke, alcohol, diet and exercise. The message is simple: cut out the fags and the ready meals; eat fresh fruit and veg; walk to work and drink more water. You'll start to look better. And better means younger.

Deep down, I think we all realise that anti-ageing cures are a waste of money. The problem is that people want to be convinced that these products have all the answers and are only too willing to lap up the scientific jargon – it's hypo-allergenic – and hokey Eastern mysticism. After all, smearing a cream on our face – especially a reassuringly expensive one – is a much easier option than going for a run. So just how stupid are we? Let me show you.

Nadine Baggot is something called a "celebrity beauty editor", and she tells me that in her job she gets to learn lots of celebrity beauty secrets. I know this because she's the star of a new advert to promote Olay Regenerist which I'm watching as I write this. Now Nadine doesn't just learn beauty secrets from celebrities – oh no – she also relies on the information she gets from beauty skin care experts to discover a few beauty secrets of her own.

To underline this fact, we now see a shot of Nadine doing just that. We can't hear what the skin care experts are saying, but one of them has glasses and Nadine is taking notes, so I bet it's something really important. Crikey! It is. And Nadine's going to tell us about it right now. You see, Nadine thinks the hottest anti-ageing ingredients around are – shit, best get a pen – pentapeptides

KTTKS. What in heaven's name are they? I wonder. Hang on a minute – what luck! Up there on the screen are the very beauty secret notes that Nadine was taking earlier on. I can see that they are tiny pieces of protein molecules that can actually help to renew the skin's surface. That's amazing! Now I don't care how it works, I just know that I want to smear the years away.

Alas, Nadine hints there might be a catch. Remember she said these were celebrity beauty secrets? Well, you'd probably expect to pay celebrity prices to get your hands on these high-tech anti-ageing ingredients, wouldn't you? I know I would. That's just the way the world is: the proles are excluded yet agai … But wait! Nadine's "discovered" that pentapeptides are available in Olay Regenerist, a moisturiser that costs only around £20 and, as she says, that's hardly a celebrity price, is it?

Even to an unreconstructed Keynesian like me, Nadine's idea that civilians should pay less for a product than celebrities seems a bit radical, but Nadine is coming across as some kind of working-class hero, stealing celebrity beauty secrets and redistributing them to the great unwashed, championing a world where the rich pay more. She's like a better-looking Denis Healey, squeezing the rich until the pips squeak.

Nadine makes it clear: she recommends Olay Regenerist because it makes her skin smoother and fuller and looking like new skin. Now that, she concludes, *is* a beauty secret worth knowing.

Given the fact that I saw this advert on prime-time television, I'm not sure whether it's all that much of a secret any more; nevertheless, I draw the only conclusion it is possible to draw from Nadine's forthright message. Clearly, Nadine has stumbled across such a big celebrity beauty secret that she must have used her own money to put an advert together and pay for it to be broadcast on prime-time TV.

And she absolutely did not say these things because she was paid to do so by Procter & Gamble. No way, José!

As I've said, it's not just you; I'm a thicko as well!

## 12 | **How Would You Get Rid of "Soap Scum, Lime-scale, Ground-in Dirt and Tough Grime"?**

Answer: There is of course only one way to get rid of "soap scum, lime-scale, ground-in dirt and tough grime", and that's to burn it off with acid.

Industrial-strength hydrochloric acid is probably best, but difficult to get hold of in the UK. It is readily available in French supermarkets, if you're ever over there, but be careful when you're using it: it goes without saying you should wear goggles and protective gloves.

Alternatively, you could use one of the many acid-based cleaners (usually a blend of two or more acids – say, citric, etidronic, sulfamic or phosphoric acid) that are on the market together with a bit of elbow grease.

I know I'm playing with fire here; I can see I'm in danger of losing you. You're probably wondering whether there isn't something more interesting on the telly, but please, bear with me, all will become clear once we consider the following questions.

First up, who on earth could possibly be interested in, let alone get excited about, acid-based household cleaners? And come to think of it, Steve, what's so useless about acid-based household cleaners anyway? Surely by their very nature they're intrinsically useful?

Reckitt Benckiser is the company behind Cillit Bang, an amazing new householder cleaner that's tough on "soap scum, lime-scale, ground-in dirt and tough grime". The people at Reckitt Benckiser are well aware that their product is very dull, but they are also aware that we are very stupid.

So when they launched Cillit Bang in the UK in 2004, they charged the advertising agency Young and Rubicam with the task of making us thickos interested in boring old Cillit Bang.

The first thing Young and Rubicam did was create a fictitious character, one Barry Scott, who would appear in all the advertising. Marketers like doing things like this; it's much easier to sell a person than a product, so their plan was to make sure Barry Scott became the brand personified. If it helps, think of Barry Scott as Cillit Bang in human form: an enthusiastic Everyman with wisdom to impart. We might not queue up for a night down the pub with him, but Barry Scott is clearly a man we'd turn to if we had a leaky pipe. And I bet he knows how electricity works. Now to make the adverts.

There are two major problems to overcome here, especially if you are trying to promote a really boring product. Most ads we see these days are very slick indeed. So slick in fact that most of them go over our heads. In a 2004 survey, consumers were shown advertisements by telecoms companies Orange and Vodafone. Over 80 per cent of those taking part had no idea what the advertisements were trying to tell them.*

Second, we've become very good at not watching ads at all. We're watching many different channels these days; it's much more difficult to get to us. And even when we are

---

* Source: MK Communications Survey for EMAP Performance, September 2004.

watching the programme you've advertised in, we may well have used our personal video recorder (PVR) to time-shift, and as such will undoubtedly have chosen to edit out your ad. And even if we're watching it live, judicious use of the remote control means many more of us have switched channels as soon as the ad break comes on.

In short, you're going to have to work like crazy to come up with something very special to catch our attention.

By these criteria, the Cillit Bang ads are works of genius. Filmed with the finesse and production values that one would typically associate with the German porn industry *circa* 1972, they begin with a bit of old-school "Where? When? Why?" straight from a marketing textbook.

"Hi, I'm Barry Scott, I'm here with Jill and I'm here to tell you about Cillit Bang …"

The effect is truly arresting: "Whatthehellisthisforreal?" is a typical response. Now he's got our attention Barry doesn't just tell us how great Cillit Bang is – he damn well shows us.

"Limescale is simply calcium carbonate that sticks. Look how Cillit Bang dissolves this solid chunk." (Close-up of Barry as he drops a chunk of calcium into a glass tank. He's right – it dissolves.)

Barry and Jill are quite friendly. "And now for the tough test," says Barry. The music and lighting might make you think they'll be taking their clothes off at any minute, but no, Barry dips a filthy penny in the same tub and it comes out sparkling bright. "You love that one, Barry!" says Jill coquettishly.

And now we're in for the shouty money shot.

"Give it a go! Bang! And the dirt is gone!"

If that wasn't enough to get us interested, we're told that we can find out more from the Cillit Bang website, which is where I head off to next.

Feeling a bit like the Omega Man, I can't help thinking that I might be the only person ever to visit this website who isn't related to either the actor who plays Barry Scott or someone working for Reckitt Benckiser. There's a section called "What people are saying", but there's nothing to qualify who these people are, and given they say things like:

> Apart from bleach, there is no need to buy
> any other cleaner, it is brilliant!

> I'm very pleased with the results of Cillit Bang
> on my oven. Got much better results than by
> using Oven Pride.

> Cillit Bang is the best thing since sliced bread!

> I'm really pleased with this product. It cleaned
> all the limescale and grime off my bathroom
> fittings and they are gleaming now.

> … Love this product – I think it's magic.

then I think it's more than likely that these unspecified "people" might well work for Young and Rubicam as well. After all, they are also responsible for the website. It's all very dull.

Clearly I should be working at Young and Rubicam because they are thinking along the same lines. Which is why, as well as the official website, they've also built a weblog – barryscottblogs.com – in what is clearly an attempt to create a viral campaign around Barry and Cillit Bang. Now, you might be forgiven for thinking that this seems a bit desperate given the anodyne nature of the product and of Barry himself: fair play to Young and Rubicam for wrangling the extra budget out of the client, but really, who's going to be interested in that?

Tom Coates is a real weblogger who runs his own site (at plasticbag.org if you're interested). For some reason Tom has decided to share intimate details of his life with others online through his weblog. He's not unique in this respect; lots of people are doing it. It's a phenomenon I don't really understand myself, but whatever helps to get you through the night, etc., and I guess it works for Tom. Anyway, on 30 September 2005 Tom posted an account of a meeting with his father – who he hadn't seen for 30 years. He invited people visiting his site to share their own experiences, and the response he received was, in his own words, "uniformly pleasant", although some were a little more emotional than he felt comfortable with. Tom was glad that everyone got something out of it.

This is one of the comments Tom received:

> Hi Tom, Always remember one thing. Life is
> very, very short and nothing is worth limiting
> yourself from seeing the ones you love. I
> hadn't seen my father in 15 years until 2 years
> ago. I was apprehensive but I kept telling
> myself that no matter how estranged we'd

become there was no river too wide to cross.
Drop me a line if I can be of any more help.
Cheers, Barry Scott

That's right, *the* Barry Scott. Barry "Bang and the dirt is gone!" Scott, Cillit Bang personified. You can't help thinking that, given that he's a fictitious character, what more help could he have possibly been? Perhaps he could have shown Tom how to get his estranged dad's coin collection not just nearly clean, but really clean? Now that would have brought them together spiritually.

And we know it was Barry Scott because Tom is a bit of a techie and he traced the computer that left the message to the offices of Young and Rubicam. Clearly Tom's a sensitive type and his weblog appeals to sensitive types. They were incensed that their sensitivities were being exploited as part of a marketing campaign and showed that often amateurs are often much better at this viral thing than the professionals by kicking up an eggy stink across the whole Web.

On 3 October 2005, Reckitt Benckiser issued the following apology:

> We are writing to you in response to the Barry
> Scott posting on 30th September 2005. We're
> all aware that Barry Scott, the advertising
> character, is a marketing creation and we have
> been responsible for raising his awareness.
> The posting on 30th September was
> unplanned and an error of judgement and we

unequivocally apologise for this. We recognise that it was inappropriate in context.

The Barry Scott character has appeared in a number of spoof websites and weblogs, created by people unconnected to the Reckitt Benckiser brand. The weblog posting on your site was not endorsed by Reckitt Benckiser or any of the advertising agencies that are mentioned and was a one off error from which lessons have been learnt. We are sorry for any offence it has unwittingly caused.

We would like to have an opportunity to apologise personally, if you would like to speak to us please do let us know the best way to reach you.

Yours sincerely,

The Cillit Bang team.*

What lessons were learned? I wonder. Is there no part of our lives that isn't considered fair game by brands and advertisers? Are we to be spared the sight of Tony the Tiger, gatecrashing somebody's funeral to say, "Listen, everyone, eat Kellogg's Frosties, they're grrrrrrrreat! And by the way: may his eternal soul rest in peace." Before chucking a handful of dirt into the grave and blasting off into the sunset, Noel Edmonds-style, in a branded hearse?

---

* "An apology from the Cillit Bang team", plasticbag.org.

Now I tell you what, *that* would get the product talked about.

One final point to make about Cillit Bang – it's all bollocks, of course.

The coin: "Bang and the dirt is gone!" Of course it's fucking gone: Cillit Bang's an acid – dip the coin in vinegar or lemon juice and the dirt will be gone.

The lump of calcium: "Look how Cillit Bang dissolves this solid chunk." Amazing. But then you'd get *exactly* the same effect if you dropped it into a bucket of water …

… as anyone who's studied chemistry at school will be able to tell you.

Shame on you, Barry!

And shame on us for being suckered into buying the stuff by the bathful.

# 13 | **How Do We Get Drinkable Water?**

There are actually two equally correct answers here.

First of all the water we get from the tap – which we drink, wash, clean our houses and cook with – is cleaned at a water treatment plant. Sometimes water is already clean when it arrives at the plant because it has been cleaned naturally by the rocks it has travelled through, which act as a giant sieve, sifting out impurities.

If the water is not already suitable to drink when it arrives at the plant, it will have to go through a cleansing process. The first stage, called screening, removes any large objects in the water. The water is sent through a pipe with gauze at the end which removes debris such as twigs, small rocks or rubbish.

This is followed by flocculation and clarification. Here chemicals are added to the water which separate it from bacteria, metals and other particles that are too small to be removed during screening.

From here, the water undergoes filtration, passing through fine sand that catches any remaining chemicals from step two.

The last step is chlorination and fluoridation. Chlorine is added to protect against any remaining harmful germs and fluoride is often added to protect drinkers' teeth. After that the water is piped under pressure to our houses. It gets through the taps by making use of capillary action: the ability of a narrow tube to draw a liquid upwards against the force of gravity.

And the second answer: you can buy exactly the same

stuff from a shop in a bottle. It's a lot more expensive, though. And I mean a lot more.

In 2006 in the UK alone we will spend an estimated £1.6 billion on over 2 billion litres of bottled water. In 1976, one of the hottest summers on record, we bought just 3 million litres and spent less than £200,000.* To ten-year-old me, water was exclusively something you got – not necessarily wanted – from a tap. Not so "the starving children of Africa".

"I'm thirsty," I'd say, and, noticing that our weekly ration of one bottle of Robinson's squash between us was now exhausted, would add, "and there's nothing to drink."

The implication was that my parents should rustle up a suitably fruity alternative, but quick as a flash Father would inevitably respond, "There's a tap full of water. The starving children of Africa would be grateful for that."

"The starving children of Africa" loomed large during this period of my childhood. I don't want to appear dismissive of world poverty and I'm well aware of the tireless work done by the international aid agencies, the fund-raising efforts of charities like Oxfam, VSO and Save the Children, the pioneering, awareness-raising triumphs of Bob Geldof and the music of Chris Martin – I'll even buy a bracelet if that's what it's going to take – but to ten-year-old me "the starving children of Africa" (a curiously singular entity) were less a totem of the systematic exploitation of the Third World by the post-imperialist Western powers, and more a bogeyman, employed by people in

---

* "Bottled Water UK", Mintel Report, 20 July 2005.

positions of authority (over me) to get me to do something I didn't want to do, or to deny me a pleasure of some description.

I would be implored to consider "the starving children of Africa" by my mum, because I declined the opportunity to feast on some particularly unpleasant vegetable, or animal part, that had found its way on to my plate; by Akela because I refused to share my ration of Opal Fruits with other members of the 45th Ormskirk Cub Scouts; and by my infants school teacher, Mrs Powell, because I was less than keen to join my classmates as they slurped their way through a carton of room-temperature milk.*

Had I been aware of the works of John Stuart Mill, I would have argued that this utilitarian approach to my own food and drink intake was making little difference to the plight of "the starving children of Africa", and that rather than offering platitudes, wouldn't it better if we all did something practical, like wear a wristband. As Chris Martin would have said/sang, "How long must they stand, with their heads in the sand?"

How long indeed.

In 1976 I was aware of bottled water. A kid in my year, Simon Mitchell, had been on holiday to Spain (he got an extra week off at Whit half-term, I remember). Upon his return Miss Rae, our student teacher, invited him to stand in front of the class and gave us a talk about this foreign land, after which we were allowed to ask questions.

---

* In 1974 I was a vocal supporter of Thatcher the Milk Snatcher, although I'm proud to say my support didn't last much beyond this. My loathing of milk remains to this day, as does my loathing of the baroness herself.

He prefaced his talk by playing a record, *El Viva España*, to set the mood. Then he pointed out where Benidorm was on the class globe. Spain, it transpired, was a strange place. Simon hadn't seen a bullfight or met any waiters called Manuel, but he did have orange juice for starters every night in the hotel restaurant and you couldn't drink the water out of the taps, you had to buy it in bottles from the supermarket. No way! But in fact, as Miss Rae, who had been to Torremolinos the year before, confirmed, very much "Yes way!"

Miss Rae explained that their water system was much more primitive than ours. Fancy that, then: water in bottles. In our minds Spain became a kind of halfway house between us fortunate British citizens with water – literally – on tap and "the starving children of Africa", who faced a round trip of 400 miles carrying a bucket on their heads to get theirs.

I first noticed the insidious rise of bottled water a few years later when I visited my Auntie Kathleen for Sunday lunch. Auntie Kathleen had recently moved to London, thereby achieving instantly a level of sophistication we provincials could only dream of, and as such the traditional Sunday roast was accompanied by a bottle of Piesporter Riesling (exclusively for the grown-ups) and a choice of lemonade or Perrier water for the rest of us. A bit like Biros or Hoovers, all bottled water at this time was called Perrier water. I decided I didn't like it. It looked like lemonade but tasted salty. It was never going to catch on.

Twenty years on and we're no closer to solving world poverty, and water shortages are becoming more popular than ever before. The south-east of England is enduring its lengthiest drought since 1976 and the problem is being exacerbated by the huge increase in population. Unlike the situation in Africa, it's more a question of maths – less water, more people – than economics.

With that in mind, can there be anything more patronising to those suffering drought in sub-Saharan Africa than the fixation of the West with bottled water? The next time Chris Martin talks about ending world poverty, quenching his post-gig thirst with a bottle of Aquafina, Evian or Dasani after putting in a back-breaking 90 minutes or so of work, he might like to consider that the answer may well be literally in his hands.

Bottled water just might be the biggest swindle in history. The cost of half a litre of tap water is about 0.03p. The same – and I do mean the same, even in the case of spring water, give or take a few trace elements of no nutritional consequence whatsoever – in a bottle will set you back about 98p. That's a mark-up of about 98p.

Bottled water manufacturers are making a fortune out of our stupidity, so it should be no surprise that the big boys want in on the action.

In April 2005 Pepsi pulled ahead of its arch-rival Coca-Cola for the first time in its history as its market cap reached $98.4 billion (£60 billion), ahead of Coca-Cola's $97.9 billion. The rise of PepsiCo has been meteoric. At the turn of the century, Coca-Cola was almost three times the size of its thirst-quenchin' rival, with a market cap of $128 billion to Pepsi's $44 billion.

But the fortunes of these two giants would not be determined in terms of cola sales – sales of fizzy drinks at both companies have been flat in developed markets since 1997. No, the critical factor in the fortunes of these two companies would be in the way they developed new brands that appealed to more health-conscious consumers: natural fruit drinks and bottled water.

Pepsi stole a march over Coca-Cola in Europe, with its Tropicana range of natural fruit juices. Coca-Cola was slow out of the blocks, and although its competitor, Minute Maid, performs well in the USA, it is as good as nowhere in Europe.

Which is why the UK launch of Dasani in 2004 was so important to Coca-Cola. As Simon Mitchell would attest, bottled water has been a ubiquitous feature of European shopping baskets for many years, born out of necessity rather than choice; we brand-conscious Brits, with our fancy plumbing, appeared to be much less of a challenge.

Most bottled water is sold at small outlets: newsagents, for example. And it was here that Coca-Cola had an ace up its sleeve. You may have noticed that most newsagents and corner shops have fridges, specially made to incorporate bottles of soda, cola or water. You'd be forgiven for thinking they had something to do with the bloke who runs the shop: an integral part of his start-up costs to provide punters like you with an ice-cool beverage. Think again. He gets the fridge for free. And who is the unseen benefactor, responsible for the distribution of this generous largesse? Take a look next time you're in the newsagent's and you might notice a big red Coca-Cola bottle – or similar – on the side of the fridge.

So when Coca-Cola announced to the retailers that:

1 We are launching a new range of bottled water called Dasani;
2 Would you be so kind as to order some and stock it in that fridge we kindly gave you a while back?;
3 And by the way, if we catch any disloyal and ungrateful retailers selling other brands of bottled water in those expensive fridges of ours, we'll think very seriously about asking for them back;
4 Don't worry about losing sales, because we'll be spending £7 million on marketing to make sure everyone is going to be drinking Dasani

unsurprisingly, the retailers fell in line and simply started ordering Dasani. Ahead of the launch, the likes of Volvic, Evian, Strathmore et al. started disappearing from newsagents' fridges up and down the land.

Of course, this didn't matter because very soon we'd be able to buy Dasani instead, which, as I've already pointed out, label notwithstanding, was exactly the same product. A fact, it would seem, that Coca-Cola knew only too well. Rather than go to the bother of finding a spring, buying a spring and building a bottling plant on it, as the European brands did, they simply did what you and I should have been doing all along: they got it out of the tap. A very big tap, granted, but a tap nonetheless.

What Coca-Cola did was to take water from the River Thames, put it through a purification process at a plant in Sidcup, very similar to the one outlined above for purifying tap water, added a few salts such as calcium chloride and bromide to give it an allegedly pleasant taste, and bang it out in labelled bottles at £1.90 per litre.

Coca-Cola marketed the product as "pure water", which was true, although "tap water" would have been more appropriate, if less catchy. When this fact was reported in the media there was a national show of indignation usually reserved only for managers of the England football team and EU food directives.

How dare Coca-Cola try to sell us something we already get for free! Did they think we were so stupid that we'd pay almost a pound for a bottle of tap water? A pound for something that is available free of charge, almost everywhere? Frankly, yes.

And then, just when Coca-Cola thought it couldn't get any worse, it did. In the midst of this PR scandal the entire UK stock of Dasani was pulled from the shelves as it was found to contain illegal levels of the carcinogen bromate. It appeared that Coca-Cola's purification process – which involved pumping ozone through the water – caused the harmless bromide to turn into bromate.

Victory for the Great British consumer was complete a few days later when Coca-Cola announced that it was delaying the relaunch of Dasani indefinitely. And we celebrated by cracking open a few bottles of water, raising them aloft in a toast and drinking to the strains of the Who's timeless anthem "We Won't Get Fooled Again". Doh!

Nothing proves we're stupid so much as bottled water. There is no medical, nutritional or scientific argument to support its consumption in preference to tap water. Economically, we're about 10,000 times worse off if we choose bottle over tap, and environmentally, when you consider the energy and effort expended in processing, bottling, distribution and disposal of the plastic containers (with a half-life of forever), it's a complete non-starter.

Perhaps Chris Martin should get a wristband made with "Tap Water Only" written on it to go with the one that says "Vote Tory".

## 14 | **Tie-breaker: Should Britain Scrap the Pound and Embrace the Euro?**

Answer: I have absolutely no idea.

I've listened to the arguments but the only conclusion I can come to is that nobody else seems to be categorically sure whether it will be a good or a bad thing. Sure, there are people arguing vehemently on both sides, but then they are the same people who were convinced that the congestion charge would lead to chaos on the roads and categorically stated that extending licensed drinking hours would create carnage in our city centres.

I might not know whether a single European currency is a good idea, but what I do know is this. Given that we don't even know how electricity works, are proud of the fact that we are useless at maths, gullible enough to drink bottled water while cleaning our coin collection and wearing a cold-cream face mask that will surely make us look ten years younger, the fact that they are going to actually ask us what we think scares the bejesus out of me.

Referendum, my arse!

On the other hand, if you don't know what to think, there are plenty of people out there who are only too willing to tell you. As we will see in the next section.

Part Three | **Mind Control**

"For better or for worse, our company is a reflection of my thinking, my character, my values."

> *Rupert Murdoch, chairman and managing director, News Corporation Ltd*

"Is there any other industry in this country which seeks to presume so completely to give the customer what he does not want?"

> *Rupert Murdoch, chairman and managing director, News International*

## 15 | **Public Opinion**

"To a philosopher all news, as it is called, is gossip, and they who edit and read it are old women over their tea."
*Henry David Thoreau, author and poet*

Cognitive Behavioural Therapy (CBT) is a process of effectively treating people suffering from pathological fears or phobias. Patients are encouraged to break overwhelming problems down into smaller parts, which makes it easier to see how the different elements – situations, thoughts, emotions, physical feelings and actions – are connected and how they are affected by them. CBT takes a lot of time – usually six months – but there is a much quicker and equally effective method of treatment. It's called flooding, and it works like this. Say you were scared of rats and you visited me, a psychiatrist who specialised in curing irrational fears by flooding. What I'd do is take you into a small room, about 8 feet square, filled with a few hundred rats. Then I'd push you inside and lock the door. When I returned an hour later, your phobia would be cured.

Flooding is not a popular treatment, but mindful that you're still coming to terms with the fact that we're all thickos, I'm going to chuck another couple of buckets of figurative rats into the figurative eight-by-eight room of your imagination.

Not only are you fundamentally stupid, but those opinions – the ones you hold so dear – well, they are almost certainly not yours either. They were put in your mind by somebody else; somebody who has a vested interest in telling you what to think. The bottom line is: you do not have a mind of your own – you are free to believe only whatever *they* tell you to.

Before we start getting paranoid, here's a fascinating statistic to cheer you up: 35 per cent of Americans get all their information about world events from celebrities. Bill Bailey the comedian told me that. Not personally – he's not a celebrity friend or anything, I just happened to be in the audience during one of his gigs.*

I presume he made it up, but the fact that a) he said it at all and b) the entire audience was happy to believe him led me to make two interesting conclusions. First, Bill Bailey's hilarious – go and see him if you get the chance. Second, it's evidently not that surprising a statistic when you think about it. Statistics plucked at random are designed to elicit one of two responses, either "Really? Well I never knew that!" (e.g., 60 per cent of students think Kate Thornton is a member of the cabinet†) or "Aha! That statistic just confirms what I've always believed to be the case" (e.g. 0 per cent of *Daily Mail* readers voted Socialist Worker at the last election).

---

* My friend Hayley was doing some work at a charity run by former Arsenal goalkeeper and TV presenter Bob Wilson. One day she took a phone call from someone trying to contact Bob. Informing the caller that unfortunately Bob was out of the office, she offered to take a message. "Just tell Bob that his celebrity friend Willie Thorne called while he was out," the caller replied. Maybe Bob knows two Willie Thornes, hence the attitudinal signifier, but not being a snooker fan during the years 1981–83, Hayley was grateful to have the caller's VIP status flagged up for her.
† I made that one up.

The British like to think that Americans are, well, a bit thicker than we are. It helps us compensate for the fact that their lives are generally so much better than ours. The USA has only one national daily paper – the anodyne *USA Today*, which is, frankly, unreadable. It pains me to say this, but anyone bemoaning the quality of the UK press should nestle down for a couple of hours with a copy of either the *New York Times*, the *Washington Post* or the *LA Times*. Take your pick; each publication is an exercise in such mind-numbing tedium that it's surprising more of their readers aren't killed by yawning themselves to death. This might be the country that gave us Woodward and Bernstein, but it is also the country that brought us 24-hour rolling news channels, despite the fact that – wars with Iraq notwithstanding – the amount of news available did not rise in proportion to the screen time this innovation made available to it. Thus, what was once comfortably delivered in a 30-minute bulletin is now spread thinner than margarine on an anorexic's toast.

If you have ever been trapped in a hotel room with only CNN or the sanitised pornography channel for company, you will know that, in terms of joy-strangling dullness and sexual content, there's often little to choose between the two. On news channels, every precious fact is commented upon and analysed. Outcomes are speculated and the speculations are in turn commented on and analysed by different experts, leaving no stone unturned, until eventually you give in and flip channels, risking $10.50 to find out whether that really is just another adult film with all the adult content taken out. It is.

The demand for content means that the definition of what constitutes news has been pushed way beyond what might be regarded as in the public interest. So is it any wonder, then, that people take the option of listening to what Oprah, Rickie or David have to say about the world instead? Gwyneth seems to know a lot about environmental issues, and isn't Keanu a Buddhist? So he must know a lot about Tibet or Asia anyway, and Tom made that film about Japan, which I expect he had to read up about ... And from here it's only a small step towards electing one of them to office, especially if they've a proven track record of, say, being tough on crime and tough on the causes of crime (*Kindergarten Cop, True Lies, Conan the Destroyer* et al.).

Rather than taking this traditionally British route of laughing derisively at the colonials and their crazy ways, I wondered just how different things are in the UK. My conclusion is, not very. Clearly this malaise is not exclusive to our stateside cousins. We live in a country where, issue for issue, *Heat, Hello!* and *OK* regularly outsell the *Guardian*, the *Independent* and *The Times*. Regardless of your definition, all these publications are sources of news, designed to keep their readers up to date and informed. Which one you buy largely depends on what constitutes news to you. To the readers of *Heat*, what Jade Goody thinks, says and does is at least as important as whatever Deborah Orr, Polly Toynbee or Julie Birchall might write for readers of their broadsheet columns.

The question is: what is news for? In *The Road to Wigan Pier*, George Orwell observes how hungry for news the unemployed people he meets on his travels are, remarking that they regularly devour entire newspapers in a single sitting. Indeed, the arrival of the morning paper was the high point of their day, or at least it was until the arrival of the evening paper, which they would similarly read from cover to cover. But to what end? They were in theory much better informed about the world, but they were, in the process, made only too aware of the ennui that dominated their own lives. It was as if the action of acquiring this knowledge served simply to highlight the hopelessness of their situation.

More recently, the *Guardian* TV critic Charlie Brooker argued persuasively in his "Screen Burn" column that part of the reason why reality TV is popular is because it provides an inconsequential version of the news for people who aren't interested in current affairs.

What news provides us with is the commodity that marketers and behaviourists describe as social currency. It provides us with the ability to engage with our peers, colleagues and friends, it is what allows us to have an opinion. The list of subjects we might want to engage with our peers about or have an opinion about is essentially unique to each of us. In my case it might be: football, music, politics and macramé; in yours it might be Jade Goody, Jordan, Westlife, the colours of the season and macramé. Guess what we'd end up talking about if we met up?

Our relationship with the media is symbiotic. If news is what sells newspapers – and funds 24-hour news channels and online news portals – so it follows that whatever will sell newspapers is news. In many ways we set the agenda, we get the kinds of news we want, but often we don't know what it is we want until we see it.

We might claim that we like good news, pictures of fluffy albino kittens and getting behind the team, but paper sales tell us the contrary is true. It is conflict which excites us. We like international disasters over which we have no control, horrendous crimes, grisly pictures, celebrity peccadilloes and infidelities, falls from grace, fraudsters and sporting failures.

But the media doesn't just tell us what is going on; it tells us what to think. It is nothing more than a vehicle for the countless organisations, businesses and individuals that are trying to do just that. It is what shapes public opinion. Our capacity to process information is phenomenal. The average UK citizen is bombarded by around three thousand messages a day. Each one of these messages – well over a million each year – is designed to change the way we think: about an issue, a person or a product.

The net result is, whether we like it or not, through our desire to keep informed we end up with opinions that are not our own.

The process of achieving this is much easier than you might think. We go through life with essentially two world views. The first is personal, compiled from information we take in through the senses in the shape of experience; the second is a broad world view, which is developed vicariously. To form a broad world view we must rely almost exclusively on – at best – second-hand or third-hand information provided perhaps by friends, peers and colleagues, but more likely by the media. The media – television, radio, print, online, etc – acts like a sixth sense, providing us with the raw information to form opinions about issues, people or subjects of which we have no first-hand experience. This opinion is further shaped and influenced through social interaction.

The problem with relying on vicarious information to form a view is that you are only ever provided with a precis (and often a precis of a precis). And moreover, a precis that you can never be certain is based on an entirely accurate source in the first place.

Compared with the richness that shapes our own personal world view, our broad world view is by nature two dimensional. We tend to see things in black and white.

For example, if you think about your circle of friends or acquaintances, then unless you're part of a religious cult I'm guessing it's fair to say that you recognise that none of them is perfect. Martin might be a very funny guy, and great company, but he is unreliable. Ian is solid, but tends to talk about golf a bit too much. Sarah is a great mum and very helpful, but can be a bit of a control freak. Hannah is very warm and gregarious, but terrible at staying in touch.

Similarly, problems and arguments with work colleagues, family or friends can often be quite difficult to solve. Most of the time no one is entirely to blame. Relationships break down for complicated reasons, so complicated, in fact, that many people resort to counselling from an impartial observer or expert to help arrive at a resolution. In short, through our experience, we understand that our lives and relationships are complex and that they cannot helpfully or easily be distilled down into component parts.

In contrast our opinions about world events, current affairs, public figures, celebrities, foreign countries and the like are stereotypes: we are for or against, they are good or bad, happy or sad. We don't like him, she's a saint, he's a crook, it would be a disaster for the country, they can't be trusted, he's a junkie, she's a liar, he's pathetic.

The strength of our opinion is typically in inverse proportion to the amount of data upon which it is based. A single gobbet of information or incident is enough. A few patronising adverts for a supermarket in 2001 was all it took to make Jamie Oliver's popularity go into free-fall. His cheeky-chappie shtick earned him an audience of over 4 million viewers for *The Naked Chef*. We bought into his pukka-patter and liked watching him whip up a post-gig risotto for his band-mates in Scarlet Division. Six months later and we'd all had enough of the fat-lipped tosser; a man prepared to whore his relationship with fiancée Jules in order sell more tons of Scottish-farmed salmon. By the time the next series of *The Naked Chef* was broadcast, he'd lost over a third of his audience.

But then came redemption. First of all he used his own money to give fifteen underprivileged kids the chance to become career chefs in the eponymous restaurant and TV show. Next, he "singled-handedly" improved the diet of the nation's children in *Jamie's School Dinners*. Now he's a hero, so much so that we'll even forgive him for giving his kids the kind of names you'd expect to hear in a Wild West bordello.*

So we see the world in black and white, but because we are almost always under- or ill-informed, while our views may be polarised, they are very rarely fixed.

---

* Poppy Honey and Daisy Boo.

For the most famous example of the public opinion U-turn, let's turn to someone who, according to her former butler at least, saw the world not in black and white, but in colour: the late Princess Diana.

If the dictionary included a definition of the phrase "couldn't care less" you'd find the following note: "viz. Steve McKevitt's attitude to the royal family".

I can't even whip up the enthusiasm to become a republican. Occasionally our paths have crossed: ten-year-old me's attendance at a Silver Jubilee street party and the visit of Prince Andrew last year to one of our clients, for example, but unless Prince Philip's doing one of his occasional and hilarious Bernard Manning impressions, I take no notice.

I'll concede, it's hard not to notice them, but I can honestly say I've never read an article about the monarchy in crisis and have never of my own volition tuned in to watch a documentary or interview about the royal family. Still, even I was shocked when I turned on the TV on the morning of Sunday, 31 August 1997 to find that Princess Diana had been killed. She seemed one of those people who go on for ever. What I didn't experience was a great outpouring of grief. What I thought was, that's very sad, she seemed like a nice person, 36 is no age to die and it's terrible news for her kids. Indeed, much the same as I would feel for anyone else I don't know who had passed away in similar circumstances.

Yet that reaction wasn't enough for the media. Over the course of the next few weeks I was repeatedly told not only that this was the saddest day of my life but exactly how I was supposed to think and behave as a consequence.

Despite the fact that there could be literally no news – there's nothing more final than death – terrestrial broadcasting was suspended so that we could be kept up to date with every single development. But there was nothing to report, no developments, just "Princess Diana continues to be dead. There will be a funeral".

TV needs pictures to tell a non-story. This led to a farcical situation whereby commentators had to fill the air with weighty and worthy dialogue while millions watched an aeroplane taxiing on the runway at Charles de Gaulle. Their attempts to imbue the situation with appropriate meaning and gravitas sound comedic today. "And there we see the plane that will be taking the body of the late Princess of Wales back to London, later today. (Pause) A Boeing 727 if I'm not mistaken. (Pause) The irony is that this was one of the Princess's favourite commercial aircraft. (Pause) The 727's safety record is second to none. (Pause) The captain, a Mr T. Spriggott of Virginia Water, Berkshire, will be hoping to maintain that record on this afternoon's flight. (Pause) Despite thirty years of flying experience, he can never have had so precious a cargo."

And so it went on. There were what felt like weeks of two-minute silences, acres of newspaper coverage, books of condolence for us to sign; even Elton John and Bernie Taupin put about 30 minutes' effort into rewriting the lyrics to "Candle in the Wind". Public spaces around royal palaces in central London became floral oceans as tributes poured in from everyone across the country. We were sad, the media told us, and this was how we should express our sadness.

One lone voice, *Private Eye*, tried to put the event into

context and railed against the media hypocrisy. It was taken off the shelves of WH Smith and Menzies for its trouble.

On the evening of Princess Diana's funeral, I was invited to a dinner at the Groucho Club, to launch the annual European Computer Trade Show at Olympia. There was actually talk of cancelling the dinner on the grounds that to celebrate on a day like this, when we were all so grief stricken, would be inappropriate.

And how does the media explain these events today? Why "mass hysteria", of course. The herd, failing to come to terms with the death of somebody they've never met, behaves like fools. My point is, in the circumstances, how were we to be given the opportunity to do anything else?

I never signed a book of condolence, never laid a wreath and observed the two-minute silences only in order to preserve the status quo. My own concerns focused on whether or not this grief might be too much for the Queen Mum. If she'd popped her clogs as well we'd have had no proper telly for a month. Shares in Blockbuster would have rocketed.

I don't believe this makes me a cold or a bad person and I'm absolutely sure I wasn't alone. But I do object to being told what to think and so should you.

There are 60 million people in the UK. I probably know a couple of thousand people well enough to remember their name, several hundred well enough to stop and chat to them if I bump into them unexpectedly, about a hundred well enough to invite to a landmark birthday party, and I am in regular contact with a few dozen. I assume I'm no exception and that your own list of friends, colleagues and acquaintances is fairly similar, which means that there are almost 60 million people in the UK whom I have never met.

Yet according to the news media, my reaction to international tragedies is dependent upon how many British people were involved. The format of these stories is always the same. The tragedy is announced: plane crashes, bomb explodes, ferry sinks; this is followed by a statement of scale: thousands dead, hundreds injured, dozens still missing; and finally there is a signifier as to how upset we are supposed to get: 50 Britons among the dead, 30 British tourists still missing. The chances are approximately 60 million to one against us knowing any of these people personally, so why are they telling us? The implication is simply that this makes it more of a tragedy. Finally, if at all possible, and just to provide a measure for our grief, a close relative of someone involved will be interviewed. Platitudes will be used to characterise the dearly departed – nobody is ever described as "a bit of a tosser" – and we will gain an even better understanding as to how we should be thinking.

On average, seven children are killed in the UK by strangers each year. How much media coverage they receive is dependent upon their ethnicity, the timing of the crime, and how photogenic the victims are. Bad news sells papers and summer is a very quiet time for news, which gives editors ample opportunity to give one of these murders – which happen on average once every two months – blanket coverage. Inevitably, the role of the police and the authorities will come under scrutiny: in the case of Ian Huntley, the question was clearly how could somebody who was tried (but let's not forget acquitted) for rape be given a job as a school caretaker? "Is Any Child Safe?" screamed the headline in the *Daily Express*.

Of course, these are terrible crimes and, of course, as much as possible should be done to protect our children. I'm all in favour of that. But while we're on the subject, what about the 103 children who were killed on the roads in 2005? Are their lives any less important? Then why don't the papers scream for a reduction in the speed limit? They are far more likely to be decrying the use of speed cameras. The fact is that scaring us rigid about paedophiles hiding behind every bush is much more likely to sell papers than telling us to slow down and drive our cars less frequently.

Figures from the World Health Organisation show that the number of children murdered in the UK halved between 1970 and 2000 from just over one hundred per year to less than fifty. Home Office figures show that 95 per cent of child murders are committed by parents, family members or guardians. Tales of abduction and murder by strangers dominate the headlines simply because they are so unusual.

And so the power of the media has a twofold effect upon public opinion. First it creates a cultural norm: a national atmosphere that guides us towards what we should think. And second, by setting the news agenda and choosing what issues to focus on, it has the effect of not only promoting those issues but, by shifting focus away from other areas, leaving little scope for alternative thought or debate.

The news is one thing, but the media's influence over our opinion isn't restricted to current affairs. This process has extended into every area of our lives. Not only do they control what we think, but what we do, say and buy.

## 16 | **You Can Think What We Like**

> "Boredom is ... a vital problem for the
> moralist, since half the sins of mankind are
> caused by the fear of it."
>
> *Bertrand Russell, philosopher*

One thing ten-year-old me would be surprised about on his
visit to 2006 is the amount of entertainment his modern
equivalents have at their disposal. In 1976 children's TV
was a couple of hours of programming in the afternoon
before Zebedee optimistically informed you it was time for
bed at 5.30 p.m. Now, of course, there are entire channels
broadcasting children's television programmes 24 hours a
day. Then there's the Internet, and mobile phones and
video games and digital radio.

The subject has been well covered. Nostalgia TV has
become a minor industry in itself, formulaic to the point of
cliché: ancient clips are linked together by rictus-grinning
minor celebrities with bed hair, "der-de-derring" the theme
tune to *The A Team* or recounting – amazingly – how they
– really, you won't believe this – used to, actually, hide
behind the sofa when *Doctor Who* was on!

I've got news for them. Television in the 1970s was shit.
The set itself represented a tantalising raft of missed opportunities and daily disappointments. For most of the day
and night it was nothing but test cards and white dots.
There was a brief flowering each evening, before it disappeared again, Cinderella-like, before the clock had struck
midnight, leaving us to wonder "What if?" What if there

were more channels? What if TV was on during the day? Or even through the night? Why didn't they just show repeats? It's not as if we had video recorders, and we'd watch anything. Often we did. We'd get up early on Sunday morning to watch *Ak Pa Hak*, hide behind the sofa during a 6.30 a.m. episode of the Open University's *Advanced Mathematics*, or try desperately to follow the plot in the dramatisations of *Parliamo Italiano*. Now in my book *that* constitutes being a telly addict.

I look at the wealth of entertainment available to my kids with envy, but while there was – often literally – nothing on worth watching, television in those days was still a deeply glamorous proposition, beyond the reach of mere mortals. To be famous, all you had to do was be on it. Appearances on TV for people I knew were so rare that I can still remember them today. The elder sister of my classmate Ian McDonald appeared on *Junior Showtime* in 1974 as one girl in a huge Morris dancing troupe. The whole school tuned in. It was all quiet for the next few years, then in 1976 not one but two memorable TV appearances happened. First up, my cousin Glen announced that he would be clearly identifiable in the audience during the forthcoming episode of *Atara's Band*, because he'd bagged a front-row seat. We tuned in; he was. Hot on the heels of this, the teacher of another cousin, Trisha, was a guest on *The Generation Game*. She even went on to win it.

I derived vicarious, but proud, pleasure in the penumbra of their limelight, so you can imagine my own excitement when, in 1975, at the age of nine, I discovered I was to be given a starring role in my own show. Clearly, television was out of my league – I didn't have the talent: I couldn't Morris-dance like Ian McDonald's sister or play "Pease Pudding Hot" on the recorder like my cousin Glen – but there was one thing I could do: I could be a cub scout. It was this serendipitous path which led me, not to TV, but to radio (surely just TV without pictures?). And not any old radio either. This was local radio. This was Radio Merseyside.

Before we start, here's a brief explanation of the radio landscape in 1975. First of all, as with TV, there wasn't much of it. There were the four main BBC channels, which to be fair were on air for longer than their TV counterparts, but, apart from Radio 4, they were available only on medium wave. This often made them all but unlistenable to by today's digital standards. Independent local radio was only just finding its feet. In my neck of the woods, the launch of 194 Radio City on 21 October 1974 had put some pressure on Radio Luxembourg, which had been enjoying free rein as station of choice for lovers of music with adverts. And finally there was BBC local radio, which was still taking its "educate, inform and entertain" mandate very seriously. So seriously, in fact, that often the "and entertain" bit deserved to appear in parentheses.

How exactly the opportunity was seized on my behalf remains a mystery to me; perhaps it was an attempt by Radio Merseyside to throw down the entertainment gauntlet to its new ILR rival. One Thursday evening at a weekly meeting of the 45th Ormskirk cub scouts, Akela announced that I had been chosen as one of a group of six cubs representing the pack on Radio Merseyside the following Sunday.

We were all beside ourselves with excitement. We were going to be famous, starring on the radio. Akela gave the details to our parents. We would be going out live on Sunday morning, for a whole hour between 6 a.m. and 7 a.m. We had to be at the station for 5.45 a.m., which meant setting off at about 5.15.

School the next day was amazing. I was blithely unaware of the concept of peak time, and so was only mildly disappointed when my dad laughed as he dropped me off, saying that our appearance was so early in the morning we'd have to make sure we spoke really quietly so as not to wake anyone up. Several of my friends asked me to mention them on the radio and promised to tune in. In fact so many people asked to be mentioned that I felt a weight of responsibility and began to worry that my starring role might consist of no more than a roll-call of my classmates. Still, I didn't want to let the fans down, and promised to do my best to accommodate them all, by listing their names ostentatiously in my notebook.

It was still dark when my brother and I were picked up by Baloo. We were suitably attired for radio in full cub-scout uniform. We were, after all, as Akela had repeatedly reminded us, representing the pack. On the way to the studio – a journey of around 18 miles – I don't think we saw more than a dozen cars, but the three of us were all very excited, full of ideas about what we were going to say, the jokes we'd tell, the stuff we'd do, the fun we'd have.

It was then I realised that I had absolutely no idea what

to expect. We'd been given no briefing other than to remember we were representing the pack, were not asked to prepare anything and indeed had been given no information about the show at all, other than when it started. I expect they just thought we'd turn up and the magic would happen.

When we arrived we were ushered into a relatively large studio. Baloo sat quietly in the corner while we were introduced to the presenter, a tall, thin woman with glasses in her late twenties. This being the 1970s, regional accents were still *verboten*, and despite this being Liverpool's only local radio station, she spoke the perfect Received Pronunciation of BBC English.

She explained that when the record finished, she'd ask us a few questions, but first could we establish a few house rules. Would we be so kind as to put our hands up if we wanted to speak? We should remember to talk clearly into the microphone and to speak only one at a time. We'd all get a chance to have a go. Then, as "Liverpool Lou" by the Scaffold faded out, the 45th Ormskirk cub scouts were broadcasting to the nation. Or at least to their immediate families and insomniacs with nothing better to do living in and around Merseyside.

This is what passed for entertainment in the 1970s. I can only imagine that even those listeners who had some connection with members of 45th Ormskirk would have been bored by the programme. To a small boy, we all froze as soon as the microphone came near us. Our interview style was firmly in the Meg Ryan on *Parkinson* mode. Questions were asked, hands stayed down. At one point my brother Paul forgot himself and gamely drivelled on about a recent family holiday in Wells, Somerset. The interviewer, thinking he'd said Wales, asked him whether he'd climbed any mountains; this had the double consequence of both confusing him and bringing home the crashing realisation that he was talking live on the radio. He immediately clammed up halfway through an anecdote about Wookey Hole swimming pool and claimed he'd spent the whole holiday in bed. I was so ashamed, not only because he had just lied to the nation* but because I was too frightened to butt in and correct him.

At one point, we were asked whether we knew any jokes. John Warburton put his hand up and said he did: "I went to an Irish restaurant last week. You could tell it was Irish: the waiters brought the soup in a basket!"

Silence.

Simon "Connors" Connelly asked why you'd get soup in a basket. John said you wouldn't, you'd get chicken in a basket, that was why it was funny. Connors told him it wasn't funny and since when did you ever get chicken in a basket? John said you got chicken in a basket in the restaurants he went to with his mum and dad and older brother, and it wasn't his fault Connors was too much of a pov to ever go to those sorts of restaurants. Nigel Perry said he'd had a chicken pie once, and the presenter said we were going to hear "Mouldy Old Dough" by Lieutenant Pigeon, and after that we'd sing a song for the people before the show finished.

We were keen to sing "Kung Fu Fighting" by Carl Douglas, and Connors said he knew all the words. Baloo

---

* Or at least to families and insomniacs with nothing better to do, etc.

immediately quashed this suggestion on the basis that he didn't think "Kung Fu Fighting" was an appropriate song for cub scouts to be singing.

And with that, an hour of top-quality audio entertainment was brought to a close and those "err-lie in the morning" listeners who hadn't drifted back to sleep were treated to a half-arsed rendition of "What Shall We Do with a Drunken Sailor" that no one really needed, or wanted, to hear.

This was my first direct contact with the media, and if the format of the programme sounds twee today, the basic premise is very much alive and well and still propping up much of the terrestrial and digital scheduling. The concept is simple: put non-professional members of the public in front of a microphone or camera and see what happens. The results will be entertaining. And there will be thousands of people willing to take part, with absolutely no idea of what they are letting themselves in for. And we'll do almost anything to get our faces in there.

In the 1980s this concept was developed further. Esther Rantzen and Cilla Black made careers out of filming working-class people looking surprised. Take an old lady from Watford out to the park. While she's gone give her a fitted kitchen and then patronise her, by filming her tears of joy and amazement when she finds out that you've got a "Heart of Gold". Now that's *brilliant* telly. Better still, find a welder from Sunderland, invite him to be a member of the audience and (surprise, surprise!) reunite him with a child he hasn't seen for 30 years. The least he can do in return is broadcast the most intimate and emotional moment of his life to 8 million viewers.

The other strand was no less cruel, but a bit more honest, and consisted of the likes of Jeremy Beadle or Noel Edmonds tricking people into believing their houses, cars or livelihoods were in jeopardy and then filming their abusive reactions.

The media has always hated the general public/civilians/the herd, and these programmes were merely the *Homo erectus* to 21st-century reality TV's fully formed *Homo sapiens*.

It's clear we hold the media in very high esteem. Many people want to be famous and the media gives them the so-called oxygen of publicity they need to achieve this. Now, over thirty years after my own broadcast debut in front of dozens of Radio Merseyside listeners, there's much more oxygen to go around, albeit mainly from digital TV and radio channels, whose audience figures will be similarly minuscule. For something that evidently hates us so much, the modern media has a frightening amount of influence over what we think, say and do. Just don't take my word for it.

The irony is that while the number of platforms, channels and publications has significantly increased since the 1970s, there has been a huge consolidation in terms of media ownership.

Back in 1976 each region had its own independent television company broadcasting as part of a network (London even had two – Thames and London Weekend Television; obviously broadcasting to the capital seven days each week was deemed to be too challenging for anyone other than the BBC). And, as we have seen, these channels broadcast for only part of the day. Most of the fledgling independent radio stations were exactly that, independent, as were local papers.

Consolidation in the media over the past twenty to thirty years has been phenomenal. One company, Carlton-Granada, controls all terrestrial independent television, competing head to head with the BBC. But even these organisations are relative minnows compared to the international media giants like Time Warner AOL or indeed Rupert Murdoch's News Corporation, which owns the Sky platforms and TV channels, Fox International and a raft of newspapers including the *Sun*, the *News of the World*, the *Herald Tribune*, *The Times* and the *Sunday Times* and HarperCollins, the book publisher.

Media is no longer a national or international business: if it's not global it's nothing. The golden opportunity for the media companies is China. A quarter of the world's population represents the single biggest market on the planet – and a relatively untapped opportunity.

There's just one problem for the free-marketers: China is still ostensibly a communist country, and despite its veneer of free-market economics and experiments with consumption, it is still a very long way from Western democracy's epitome of freedom. It's not simply enough to brush its appalling human rights record, systematic persecution of dissidents, or illegal occupation of Tibet to one side during business negotiations – especially not if you're a media corporation, pumping out negative stories about the regime on a regular basis.

The media moguls have been forced not just to bend

over backwards, but to bend over forwards to accommodate the wishes of the Chinese government. Disney, for
example, created a full-length animated feature, *Mulan*,
which was expressly targeting the Chinese market. Based
loosely on a Chinese legend, *Hua Mulan*, the central character was a departure for Disney: neither a princess nor
regarded as beautiful. The film itself is highly sympathetic
to the Chinese regime and had the dual purpose of promoting Disney in China – where it was something of a flop,
audiences not warming to Mulan's Westernised complex-
ion and appearance – and positively promoting China to
the rest of the world. The kind of bold ambitions, one
imagines, that would have made Leni Riefenstahl proud.

Indeed, a positive portrayal of China is paramount to
all the major media corporations hustling for position like
queue members in *The Annabel Chong Story*. On 27 February 1998, the *Daily Telegraph* reported that Harper-
Collins was planning to drop its publication of a memoir
by former Hong Kong governor Chris Patten on the
instructions of Rupert Murdoch's global media group
because it contained strong criticism of China. There was
also allegedly "an understanding" among News International reporters that there was to be no negative coverage
of the UK visit of Chinese prime minister Hu Jintao in
April 2005.

Whether there was an understanding or not, there was
definitely no negative coverage of the visit.

## 17 | **The Extension Trip**

> "Suppliers and especially manufacturers have
> market power because they have information
> about a product or a service that the customer
> does not and cannot have, and does not need
> if he can trust the brand. This explains the
> profitability of brands."
>
> *Peter Drucker, economist*

Brands will do anything to get you to buy their product. Don't blame them – they have to. Sure, they know we're stupid, that we'll believe anything and that our opinions are easily shaped and moulded, but unfortunately so do their competitors.

This is why brands try to ride the Zeitgeist as much as possible. In 2004 McDonald's famously decided that they were going to offer fresh fruit and salads to their customers. This move, they claimed, had nothing to do with the Morton Spurlock movie *Supersize Me*, popular non-fiction titles *Junk Food Nation* and *Fatland* or the weight of newspaper articles highlighting the unhealthy nature of the Big Mac that appeared the same year, but was simply a response to customer demand for healthier meals. How altruistic of them.

In May 2006, during the run-up to the World Cup, McDonald's announced that it was scrapping its healthy options, because no one was buying them, and was introducing a 33 per cent bigger Big Mac.*

---

* *Sunday Times*, 15 May 2006.

I wasn't surprised. In 2000 I had a meeting with a senior marketer at McDonald's UK who explained their business model to me in his own words: "It's quite simple. If you buy one burger at McDonald's, we want you to buy fries and a Coke. If you visit once a week, we'll persuade you to visit twice. Come on your own? We want you to bring a friend or your family. Upselling, that's what we're all about."

The individual no longer works there, so before the McDonald's litigation team reaches for the phone, can I just say I don't know whether this is still the business model and I've only got his word that it ever was. But what I can say is this – think about it. What else could they possibly be trying to do? Getting us to buy fewer burgers? Why do they have to be responsible? They already tried that and it didn't work.

The fact that some of the unhealthiest brands spend the most money sponsoring sport has been well documented. As I write, Pringles, McDonald's and Coca-Cola can all be found leveraging their involvement with the World Cup 2006.

The question is: why do they do this? Coca-Cola has been sponsoring the World Cup since 1978, but nobody associates the brand with a sporting and healthy lifestyle. Even less so McDonald's or Pringles.

It's a question Sergio Zyman, the chief marketing officer of Coca-Cola, asks in his book *The End of Marketing – As We Know It*:

> Associated imagery, like the other elements of
> marketing, has to stem from and be grounded

in strategy ... Why does Coke sponsor soccer?
You should only associate yourself with
something if you have a strategy, and a reason
for doing it, not because your competition is.
Pepsi's choice to ally with Michael Jackson
and Lionel Richie did not sway Coke to do
the same thing and for good reason.

There is a dearth of ideas in the FMCG sector for good reason. The brands are running out of ideas and failure has become a dominant feature: 85 per cent of new product launches in the FMCG sector fail. Rather than innovate, product managers have followed a strategy of selling us "the same, but different". It's called a brand extension.

The brand leaders know that we have mixed feelings when it comes to brands. We think they are overpriced and rely too heavily on marketing and promotion. On the other hand we find them aspirational and associate them with high quality.

The brand extension is a hedge-your-bets strategy that works on the assumption that if you like product X you might be more easily persuaded to buy product X-plus rather than product Y.

For example, let's say you're a fan of KitKat; then we might find it easier to get you to try a chunky version of the bar than a completely new brand you've never heard of before. And not just easier, but less expensive.

The science behind brand extensions is rather simple and you don't have to take an MBA to understand how they work.

The research tells us that if you launch a brand extension then you will not need to spend anything like as much money on marketing as you would for a completely new product, because customers will make a lot of assumptions based on their experience of the parent brand. You can therefore cash in on all the goodwill – or equity – that exists for the parent brand.

Let's pretend you're a fan of Ben and Jerry's ice cream. One day you're out shopping and you see a new product of theirs, not an ice cream, but a frozen yogurt. Immediately you would make a number of assumptions about the frozen yogurt. You would expect it to be relatively expensive in comparison to other brands of frozen yogurt, to perhaps have a funny name and to be a purchase for special occasions rather than an everyday one. If you're in the market for a frozen yogurt, you'd probably plump for this one.

So far, so good, but there is a catch – isn't there always? – and it's this. Brand extensions work only when the extension has a strong connection with the values of the parent brand. If you launch into a sector that doesn't work so well, the original brand actually has a negative effect.

Again, let's pretend you're a fan of Ben and Jerry's ice cream. One day you're out shopping and you see a new product of theirs, not an ice cream, but a range of training shoes. Now you're confused, because you always associated Ben and Jerry's with ice cream and you've no idea why anyone would want to use that brand on training shoes. You've got absolutely no intention of buying them.

Often the connections are not clear on first examination, and this is where the skill comes in.

Take Adidas deodorant or Camel and Marlboro clothing – it's not initially clear why these should be successfully spun out of sportswear and cigarettes. In the case of the deodorant, one can see that if Adidas are experts at kitting us out for sport and exercise, it's not a mental leap of faith to think they might have some expertise in freshening us up afterwards. For cigarette brands, we have to go back to the 1970s for the answer, when many more people smoked. In those days, when you placed your packet of smokes on the table, you were making a statement about yourself. You were a Marlboro, Rothman's or Stuyvesant man; a Pall Mall, Regal or Silk Cut woman. It's a relatively small step from here to wearing the clobber.

Of course, the world of brand extensions is littered with glorious failures: *Cosmopolitan* yogurts, Harley-Davidson cake decorating kits and new *Pink Panther* movies starring Steve Martin.* But the problem isn't with the failures, it's with the successes.

Brand extensions dominate the supermarket aisles and shelves. Once upon a time there was just Persil – now there's biological, non-bio, gel, liquid, powder, tablet, colour, whites.

Recently I went into the shops to buy a bar of chocolate. Getting to that age where a moment in the mouth means a lifetime on the waistline, I decided to take the faux-healthy option of buying a Wispa (on the basis that a bar consisting of half air/half chocolate must be twice as healthy as a similar-sized bar that is all chocolate).

---

* You'd think he'd have learnt his lesson after *Sergeant Bilko*, wouldn't you?

The Wispa bar was launched by Cadbury in the mid-1980s. The memorable TV campaign featured *Yes Minister* stars Paul Eddington and Nigel Hawthorne whispering to each other (see what they did there?) in close-up against a blackout: their participation alone presumably gobbling up almost the entire production budget. Ever since, Wispa has been a stalwart of my calorie-controlled diet. Alas, in August 2003 Cadbury withdrew the Wispa bar for ever, replacing it with a "same but different" extension of its Dairy Milk brand.

"So what?" I hear you cry. Well, the thing is, companies like Cadbury don't make decisions like this on the fly. To get from Wispa to Dairy Milk Bubbly will have been a very lengthy journey, one that will have involved internal brainstorming, briefings to various creative, advertising and branding agencies, internal and external focus-group testing, proposals for packaging, and undoubtedly extensive PR and advertising campaigns to communicate all these changes to the end user, i.e. me and Wispa fans everywhere.

All this effort for what? To give us KitKat that is slightly different from the one we had last week. Brand extensions have made consumer choice an illusion. Tesco, for example, is no longer just a supermarket, it's a bank, an insurance broker, a mobile phone operator and a music download platform.

The brands try to wrap their tentacles around every aspect of our lives. *Kerrang* was once nothing more than a music magazine for metalheads until its brand owners, EMAP, decided it was in fact about "anything to do with a guitar", and spun out a digital TV channel, a digital radio station, local analogue radio stations, live events and compilation albums. While none of these has been what you would call an unqualified success, the example of *Kerrang* is indicative of brands' desire to "own" our hobbies and passions because this is where we choose to spend our disposable income and is what we get most emotional about.*

And an emotional customer with money is the most easily manipulated of them all.

---

* A few words of advice for marketing people: whenever you are in a meeting to discuss brand extensions, some dickhead will always pipe up: "But what about brand dilution?" If you can't kill them, just ask them what they mean. They won't know, at which point you can smile and say reassuringly: "Don't worry. It's not our intention to get this wrong."

## 18 | **The Global Village Idiots**

**Village idiot** *n* person well known in their community for stupidity or ignorant behaviour. The term first appears in *Major Barbara* by George Bernard Shaw. The supposition is that in every small rustic town, there resides a dimwitted individual whom his fellow denizens regard as very amusing.

**Global Village** *n* metaphor to describe the World Wide Web, which allows users from around the world to connect with each other. This new reality has implications for forming new sociological structures within the context of culture.

"Where is East Angular [*sic*], is it abroad?"
*Jade Goody, millionaire*

We are drones, tiny units of production that have lost the capacity for original thought. Our opinions, tastes and attitudes are shaped by a cabal of corporations whose business objective is to sell us a homogenised version of the world. We eat the same, drink the same, dress the same, believe the same. The promise of choice is an illusion: we are free to think only what we are told and believe what they tell us is true ...

I'm aware that I'm starting to sound paranoid (and remember, even if I was paranoid it wouldn't mean they aren't out to get you), and if that's the case I feel that this might be a bit hypocritical of me. Even if what I've said is true – and I believe that it is – that doesn't mean I'm writhing around in a vat of home-brewed misery and despair. Far from it – I love my life.

When my last book, *City Slackers*,* was published, interviewers would inevitably ask whether I was a grumpy old man. The answer is always no, I'm not. It's a concept I particularly dislike, and I feel embarrassed for the people involved with that particular brand of books and TV shows. I can forgive John Peel anything, but middle-brow clowns like Tony Hawke, whose "career in comedy" started with a comedy record about stuttering under the nom de plume Morris Minor and the Majors and went rapidly downhill from there, getting worked up about why Baron's Court has an apostrophe when Earls Court doesn't deserve to be made to travel around Ireland with a fridge. A fridge filled with shit. With a bomb in it.

I'm too happy to be grumpy. Without wishing to sound smug, I've got a fairly interesting job, work with a good bunch of people, have a good circle of friends, and enjoy family life. I'm also proud to say I enjoy popular culture. I just think that things could be better than this. Much better. I believe that we could live in a happier, less exploitative world, where the pinnacle of human achievement isn't a ready meal, where people aren't lied to by advertisers, told what to think by the media or duped into

---

* *City Slackers* is a book I wrote about people who build very successful careers without ever achieving anything. It's available in "selected" retail outlets, i.e. those bookshops that "selected" it rather than those we selected.

buying snake oil by a future monarch. And one day I'm going to get round to really doing something about it. Just as soon as the World Cup finishes. Actually, the latest series of *Big Brother* takes us through to the start of the new season, so I might leave it until next year. Depending on what kind of start Wigan Athletic make and whether the third series of *Lost* is available to download by then.

The Roman emperors understood that to ensure law and order in an empire containing 70 million souls and covering much of Europe, Asia Minor, the Middle East and Africa, you had to keep the punters happy. The 1 million citizens of ancient Rome didn't have much work to do, but they still needed feeding and entertaining, and you'd be providing the money for bread and circuses out of the imperial purse if you wanted to make sure they would behave themselves. Handouts and entertainment were provided gratis to ensure a malleable population. Clearly not all the emperors were happy about this. At the end of one particularly memorable games, Gaius Caligula Caesar rose to accept the adulation of the crowd. With the cheers ringing out, he turned to one of his retinue and said mournfully, "Would that the Roman people had a single neck."

Even today, bored people become restless people. Karl Marx may once have noted that "Religion is the opium of the people", and while that remains true for many parts of the world – not least Middle America – in the secular West the drugs don't work as well as they used to. What would Karl have made, I wonder, of reality TV?

Reality TV is serving television well. In fact it's a Holy Grail of a format: it's very cheap to produce, capable of generating hours and hours of programming, delivers massive audiences and fuels its own publicity. Furthermore, it represents the kind of cross-platform content that New Media heads are so keen to commission. Cross-platform entertainment is just industry-speak for a brand extension, in other words a series that has more to it than what you watch on the screen. In the case of *Big Brother*, for example, there is the terrestrial TV show, the digital TV shows, the website, and voting via mobile and news updates available by text, WAP or email. There's even a celebrity variant. All these items are extensions of the parent Big Brother brand and all of them are capable of generating additional revenue.

And generate huge amounts of revenue they do, because the audience's appetite for reality TV seems insatiable. *Big Brother* is now in its seventh year and there's no sign that audiences are going to get bored soon. The format is familiar and comforting, but a brand-new cast is introduced every year. The performers are willing to give up everything for a relative pittance in return. The winner might get £100,000 – the equivalent of a week's work for Thierry Henry or Wayne Rooney – but he or she is the only one who'll be remunerated financially. Or at least, the only *contestant* who gets any money. Endemol, the production company behind *Big Brother*, turned over £97.3 million in the UK alone in 2004. In the same year, Peter Bazalgette, the UK chairman, earned over £4.5 million.*

By way of compensation, the contestants do have the

---

* *Financial Times*, 11 August 2005.

prospect of instant fame to console them, which is presumably why they take part in the first place.

Get on to local radio and sing "What Shall We Do with a Drunken Sailor" and, as we've seen, your family and friends would be falling over themselves to tune in – many of them discovering for the first time that there is a 6.30 in the morning as well.

I talked about my local radio appearance for years afterwards.* Not ostentatiously, you understand, but certainly when talk turned to the media, I was only too willing, like Prince Charles, to bring the wealth of my inconsiderable experience to bear upon it.†

You'll have to do more than get on local radio to impress anyone today. Even your own series on terrestrial TV is no guarantee of lasting celebrity. Take the residents of the *Big Brother* house. Each year, a set of nonentities are turned into superstars overnight and, purely by dint of sharing a flat together, they also take over the news agenda for the duration of the programme, effectively dividing the nation into two camps: those who follow the show and those who pretend they don't.

Channel 4 and its digital brand extensions E4 and More4 will dedicate hundreds of hours of programming to what they label a "social experiment".‡

The tabloid press, ignoring the fact that these are real people (because it's not as if we made them go in, is it?),

---

* You could say I'm still doing it today.

† And you could say I'm still doing this as well.

‡ An experiment with no purpose, method or measurable results. So not an experiment at all, then.

arbitrarily decide who are the goodies and baddies and then fish about in their private lives with the thoroughness and sensitivity of Spanish trawlermen. Former classmates are approached via friendsreunited.com and a hotline number is placed in the newspaper; indiscretions and peccadilloes are described in forensic detail.

The broadsheets will tut and shake their heads in disapproval, but at the same time will dedicate acres of snooty coverage to the fact that the tabloids are dedicating acres of coverage to such a puerile and meretricious entertainment. Even at work, we can log on to the *Big Brother* website to find out what our virtual friends are up to.

And for what? Like candyfloss, *Big Brother* and its contestants quickly melt away into nothing. Once they are out of the house, the contestants go back to being normal people – slightly unhinged in some cases perhaps, but normal people none the less, regardless of whatever crazy stuff they got up to on the show.

We shouldn't be so surprised. The contestants are entertaining, but they are not entertainers. The stoicism of Tom, the dull Irish farmer, may have been a laudable quality as he sought to mediate between factions caught in a life-or-death struggle over inappropriate use of the cruet, but take him out of the house and he's a dull Irish farmer. Not someone we'd want to be trapped in a lift with, let alone watch on real telly.

For most contestants the zenith of their ambition is to become a TV presenter. As I've said, the media really does hate civilians, and never more than when they are getting delusions of adequacy. The achievements of *Big Brother* alumni in this regard are a stern reminder of this, exercises in cruelty akin to meeting a man dying of thirst and offering him a cup of stale piss to drink.

Supping most gratefully is Alison Hammond – think Rusty Lee minus the culinary skills – who enjoyed a stint on *This Morning* and now presents a you-could-win-£10,000-by-answering-this-question style quiz on ITV Play.

Challenging her for a gulp of this refreshing draught are two former winners: Brian Dowling, a gay stereotype who has become a children's entertainer, and Kate Lawler, who was drafted in when it was clearly too late to save Channel 4's disastrous breakfast show *Rise*. Further back in the queue are original series winner and runner-up Craig Phillips and Anna Nolan. The chirpy Scouse chippy presented a DIY show on a digital TV channel which I know for a fact you've never ever seen. He was also the non-ironic figure of fun on godawful *Bo'Selecta*. Former nun Nolan has found fame of a sort in her native Ireland after her Louis Theroux-style vehicle *Anna in Wonderland* was quickly dropped by the BBC. She now presents *The Afternoon Show* on RTE.

Licking the cup dry is Caroline O'Shea, who appeared fleetingly in the first series, and is to be found anchoring a show on Legal TV, a channel dedicated to making the law more accessible to the general public, or more specifically the dozen or so whose batteries on their remote control died as they were rifling up through the channels in search of something else to watch.

The one exception to this rule is of course Jade Goody.

The ubiquitous Jade is the epitome of success with the absence of achievement. It's as if Jade has gathered up all the broken hopes, dreams and ambitions of every other *Big Brother* contestant ever, gambled them on red and now just can't stop winning.

Even during her time in the house there was little sign that Jade was going to buck the trend. By the time the series reached its midpoint, she was being branded "The Pig" by the *Sun*, and escaped eviction thanks only to some eviction rule changes. The tabloids also informed us that the nation was aghast at her regular displays of stupidity. Here was somebody who thought that Rio de Janeiro was a person, that Portugal was in Spain and that the "eyes" in peacock feathers really were eyes. Even the caring, sharing, soar-away *Sun* seems to have had a crisis of conscience when the British public, having been programmed how to think, started displaying effigies and banners screaming "Kill the Pig". Despite a minor turnaround in her popularity, Jade didn't win – she didn't even come second – but it's fair to say this was the last time she was ever a loser.

Four years on and Jade is without doubt a major star. A veteran of further own-reality TV shows – *Jade's Salon* and *Wife Swap* – she regularly appears on chat shows giving her opinions on important events of the day; is never out of the gossip pages of newspapers or women's magazines; and her biography is top of the book charts, enjoying sales beyond the wildest dreams of most writers (me included, and I have had some pretty wild dreams in my time, I can tell you).

Jade is launching her own range of perfume, has given

hope to fat people everywhere by bringing out her own exercise video,* and now runs her own company. She's a millionaire.

The interesting question in all this is: why? Why is she so successful? She's got no talent. She doesn't even "present," which is surely the entertainment equivalent of learning how to chew your food before you swallow. In fact the best I can say is she's quite smiley and seems like a very nice person, but then so does the girl who works in our local chippy, so I don't think that in itself is a recipe for millionaire stardom status. Also, Jade's celebrity seems to come effortlessly; in stark contrast to the stage-school demands for attention that mark out the likes of the easier-on-the-eye but arguably even more vacuous Mylene Klasses of the world. At least one could argue that Jade is being herself.

And herein lies the answer, because – let's be honest – what a very dim self it is.

If there has been anything consistent about Jade's rise from pig to pig-in-muck, it has been the reports of, to put it politely, her naivety. We're given to understand that Jade might be rich, but, hey, what a dur-brain!

In 2006 the *Sun* reported that when a "friend" had helped him or herself to over half a million quid of Jade's money, it took her six months to notice. Also in 2006 Jade tried to run the London Marathon – for charity, of course, or as Jade herself put it in a *Sun* exclusive, "to erase wareness" – despite doing no training whatsoever. She col-

* Not, I should point out, hope that they can get thin, but hope that they might one day star in their own exercise video.

lapsed after 18 miles and pictures of the corpulent star wrapped in a tinfoil cloak, looking more oven-ready than Olympic-ready, appeared in all the national newspapers. In fact her ignominious failure garnered significantly more coverage than any of the winners.

So, she's no athlete, she's not a presenter, she doesn't perform, and even in the shallow world of celebrity you'd be hard pushed to suggest that her face is her fortune. But Jade does have a skill, one that she's exploited, albeit unknowingly, to great effect. Quite simply, Jade makes people feel good about themselves; by providing a very low benchmark, she makes it very easy for them to achieve a positive comparison.

It's a cultural phenomenon with a rich cultural heritage. In crueller, or less media abundant, times we may well have got the same kicks from queuing up to jeer at the village idiot. There is a long history of people achieving considerable fame and notoriety based on providing a context, or measure, against which the whole audience will judge themselves to be superior. Perhaps the most successful exponents of this art in modern times were Laurel and Hardy.

Stan Laurel was a considerable star in his own right when studio boss Hal Roach paired him with archetypal heavy Oliver Hardy, in the final years of silent film.

British-born Laurel was a consummate professional. He had served his apprenticeship in the British music hall before going to America in 1919 as Charlie Chaplin's understudy. Indeed, Laurel had dreams of replicating Chaplin's success as an auteur, writing, directing and performing his own material, so he was initially very hostile to the involvement of Hardy. Oliver Hardy was an amiable but seemingly unsophisticated movie man who preferred spending his time on the golf course to honing his art.

Despite Laurel's misgivings, they went on to be the most successful double act of all time and the first international comedy stars of the talking-picture era.

Popular history has Laurel down as the comedy genius, but many believe it was Oliver Hardy who came up with the idea for their characters. Stan played the stupidest person on the planet; Ollie's character was ostensibly much more articulate than Stan's, and certainly considered himself to be much smarter, but in truth he was just as dumb underneath. From this simple set-up some of the best comedy in history was derived, albeit with a little help from superb acting, writing, directing and timing. Few of us will know anyone as dense as Stan, but we can all relate to Ollie's character and his pompous lack of insight – the inspiration for a host of great comic characters from Inspector Clouseau, Captain Mainwaring and Basil Fawlty to Delboy Trotter and David Brent.

Laurel and Hardy understood how to use pathos and bathos. During the 1930s depression, cinema audiences flocked to see them. Their appeal was simple. No matter how bad things were for you, at least they weren't as bad as they were for Laurel and Hardy: their plans, relationship and business ventures were doomed to failure, their hopes and dreams destined to remain so for ever, from the second they were conceived. By playing the ultimate losers, they understood how to make people feel better about their own lives and situations. This insight shows why their films are still funny today, when others – like Chaplin before them or Abbott and Costello after – have become quaint period pieces with no connection to modern audiences.

The difference is, of course, that Laurel and Hardy were fictitious characters, while Jade Goody is a real person. Hers is a much crueller variety of fame, and she has more in common with the drivelling halfwit brought out on special occasions so that the "normal" population might laugh at them than with two of the greatest comic actors of the twentieth century.

In May 2006 a new series began on UK Living: it's a fly-on-the-wall documentary about Jade's latest business venture, *Ugly's Beauty Salon*. I'm guessing that the production team aren't looking forward to delivering a textbook case study of how to start a business. I think they might be expecting that things will go wrong and are looking forward to filming them. Cynical old me? Well, Jade herself predicts in the publicity bumph that we'll get to see her "bumps an' all".

If you breed a goose that's genetically preconditioned to eat grain until its stomach bursts and its liver turns to foie gras, does that make the resulting pâté any less morally reprehensible?*

Suggest to anybody that they are less intelligent than Jade Goody and I guarantee you'll be looking at somebody who's mortally offended. In episode one of *Just Jade*, we see the

---

* But undeniably delicious all the same.

show's star discussing the redecoration of her boudoir: "I think I'm the Queen in my bedroom – I've got gold bedding and the biggest mirror in the world above my bed."

What the Queen and Phil the Greek are doing with a mirror over their bed is anyone's guess. Perhaps Jade knows something we don't ... actually, that would be impossible, wouldn't it?

Jade's role is to provide us with a measure against which we cannot fail to excel. Jade provides us with a guilty pleasure: here, the media tells us, is a human being we cannot help but feel superior to: "Why are we so interested in this nobody? [and when they say "we" they really mean "you']. Turn to pages 4, 5, 7, 10–13 and 17 to find out."

The purpose of this peculiar kind of modern celebrity, by which I mean the much-maligned concept of simply being famous, is twofold. First, it provides the media with content; when there isn't enough real achievement to go around, simply invent your own. And second, it serves to put our own lives into context: better looking than him, not as clever as her, smarter than them, worse dressed than us. Perhaps you think I've been cruel, and certainly fellow celebrity idiots are quick to point out how much more money she's got than I have – as if accrual of wealth is some sort of guide to intelligence (witness the royal family, especially Prince Charles, several lottery winners, Victoria Beckham, etc.). And if you're metaphorically armed with a shotgun and confronted by a large slow-moving target, it's difficult to stop yourself taking potshots.

The comparatively tiny number of TV hours available for ten-year-old me to watch were filled with people who were there only because they were patently cleverer than you or I were ever going to be. In the 1970s David Bellamy, David Attenborough, James Burke, Kenneth Clark, Jacob Bronowski, Desmond Morris, Patrick Moore, the Magnuses Pyke and Magnusson, Marion Davies, Carl Sagan and even Miriam Stoppard were scientists, doctors and boffins who could regularly be found on prime-time television. Today, only Attenborough still has a similar presence, and nobody has come in to replace the rest.

You can play your David Starkeys and Simon Schamas all you like; in response I'll simply say this. In 2004 BBC Online ran a survey to find the nation's most popular TV scientist. The winners, with over one third of the vote, were Dr Bunsen Honeydew and his laboratory assistant Beaker. For those of you who don't know, they are stars of *The Muppet Show*. The pair, whose experiments usually end with Beaker being blown up, were chosen to mark the British Association's Festival of Science. Eruditely summing up the concerns of the scientific community, who had conceived the festival and the survey as a vehicle to promote the responsibility of being a scientist, Dame Julia Higgins, then head of the BA, said, "I'm not sure that Dr Honeydew is quite the role model we would be looking at for a responsible scientist."

And do you know what? Neither am I. But guess who they beat into third place: could it have been theoretical physicist Stephen Hawking? Or maybe Sir David Attenborough (not a scientist really, but he's undoubtedly made a major contribution to popular understanding of natural history)? Or perhaps even the controversial evolutionary biologist Richard Dawkins? No, it was in fact Mr Spock, the first science officer of the Starship *Enterprise*.*

Celebrity imbeciles are a curiously modern combination. *Heat* magazine, that weekly circle-jerk of misanthropic *Schadenfreude*, can't decide whom it hates more: the Z-list celebrities gasping for the oxygen of publicity within its pages or its readers clamouring for a regular fix of lives allegedly less ordinary, like slobbering serfs gazing through the castle windows at the lord's Christmas feast.

*Heat* and all the copycat magazines, newspaper columns and television programmes it has spawned offer their audience nothing more than envy and self-loathing. Like Class A drug users, we might know it's bad for us but it offers us the release that while things might not be going that well, at least we're not that stupid. And if they can do it, why can't we? Tantalisingly, lives lived between the pages of *Grazia* magazine are made to seem notionally achievable and an empirical aspiration. If reality TV is the Ritalin of the people, then celebrity is the crack cocaine.

But we're not uncomfortable with this state of affairs. Far from it – while we might not be exactly happy, just as long as the illusion of choice is maintained, so we can get what they tell us we want, when we want it, we're unlikely to kick up a fuss. The less effort we put in, the more we think we should get out. After all, if Jade's got it, then why can't we?

---

* To add insult to injury, the news item announcing the results on the BBC website referred to "*Star Trek*'s Doctor Spock". Any fool knows, of course, that Dr Spock is in fact a real scientist who wrote several books about developmental psychology.

Part Four | **Everything Now!**

"You can never get enough of what you don't need to make you happy."
*Eric Hoffer, US social philosopher*

"God forbid that India should ever take to industrialism after the manner of the west ... keeping the world in chains. If [India] took to similar economic exploitation, it would strip the world bare like locusts."
*Mahatma Gandhi, political leader*

## 19 | **At Your Convenience**

> "In the kingdom of consumption the citizen is king."
>
> *Raoul Vaneigem, Situationist*

So we don't know what we want, but we sure as hell know when we want it. And we might not care if it's any use, just as long as we can get our hands on it now. Ten-year-old me would concede that life in 2006 takes place at a frenetic pace, and while technology hasn't given us space travel and jet packs it has definitely made shopping easier.

Virtually all the content ever created is available for instant access via the nearest PC, iPod, PSP, MMS phone or iTV. Consumers know that if they press a button, something will happen; and 8-meg connections to the Internet will make sure they aren't drumming their fingers while it happens.

The entertainment industry is not so much wrestling with the future challenge of new distribution channels as hiding in the cupboard under the stairs and shitting its pants at the very thought of it.

Music industry executives, for example, can be divided into three categories. First, there are those who console themselves that hard media, like DVDs and CDs, still account for the majority of sales and that downloading is a problem for the future rather than today – the Doves. Then there are some who believe that downloading is the biggest threat to the music industry – or at least its profits – and needs to be at worst controlled and at best stamped out completely – the Hawks. And finally, there is another group that believes a new market is emerging which will increase consumer choice and ultimately lead to the democratisation of music – the Clowns. It's the same in every industry.

What the clowns fail to realise is that customer choice isn't the purpose of competition. Winning is the purpose of competition. Bill Gates knows this better than anyone. The history of the Microsoft Corporation is a series of competitions from which they have emerged victorious. The process started 30 years ago with victory over IBM, and has continued without abatement. The battle for video game console supremacy with Sony is just one contest, in a war taking place on many fronts. If there were any losers left, they would tell you a Microsoft victory is always total.

In the mid-1990s anyone surfing the Internet would almost certainly be using a browser called Netscape Navigator. Version 3.0 of Netscape Navigator was ubiquitous, and its parent company, Netscape Communications Corporation, had a healthy market value of $800 million. Not huge by multinational corporation standards, but big enough, one suspects, to keep its owners in buns.

The unique feature of Netscape's web browser was that it brought consistency to the online experience. Today, when we visit a particular website, we expect it to be the same no matter what computer we view it on. It was Netscape which pioneered this user experience.

Microsoft viewed the success of Netscape as a major threat, and so to "compete" it decided to give its own web browser, Internet Explorer (the one that you almost certainly use, along with 96 per cent of the population), away free with copies of its Windows operating system. Netscape simply couldn't compete and was eventually taken over by AOL, where it remained as a software brand. By May 2006, according to AOL, only 1 per cent of PC users were using its Mozilla Firefox (Netscape 8.0) browser.

Now *that's* a competition. Not a fair competition, I'll grant you, but one in which there were clear winners and losers. And, as my mum was always keen to emphasise to ten-year-old me, life's not fair. In the world of football, Chelsea operate a similar strategy to that of Microsoft, paying not so much for success as the complete extermination of the possibility of failure. The best teams in the world are now Chelsea and Chelsea reserves.

In many ways the concept of choice is very similar to the concept of charity. I've long found it amazing that you can get away with almost anything as long as it's done for charity. It's astonishing how many Z-list celebrities will offer their time on an "expenses only" basis in return for little more than blanket publicity.*

When I was a student at Sheffield University, we tried to get the *Rag* mag banned. Our prosecution was based on the fact that it was racist and sexist (bear with me here, I'm not going to go all "Cuba" on you – it was the 1980s). *Rag*'s defence was based entirely on the fact that the mag raised a lot of money for charity and that proceeds went to a good cause. Technically one reason, then, we pointed out, and more to the point, a "cause" that few people laughing at the gags about "wogs and darkies" would

---

* Except that often it's not "expenses only" at all. Many celebrities are paid a straight fee, which is known as an "honorarium".

know or care anything about. Sensing that we were winning the intellectual battle, *Rag* got a woman up to tell a joke about two nuns and a dildo (thus proving she wasn't offended), which got big laughs, and our defeat was complete. Our loss was charity's gain.

Raising money for charity is much more sophisticated in the 21st century. The process of paying a direct debit from your bank account to a charity of your choice, pushing your loose change into a collecting tin or running off a few thousand mags containing off-colour jokes just isn't enough. Before we make a donation we have to sit gratefully through hours of "entertainment" consisting of celebrities in juxtaposed roles. BBC newsreaders do the hokey-cokey on *Children in Need*, some bloke from a reality TV show rows naked across the Atlantic, a comedian reads the news, soap stars tell jokes, sportsmen and women perform Shakespeare, Paul Burrell eats some dead mice, and Paul Daniels and Debbie McGee perform a memorable rendition of the Fall's "How I Wrote Elastic Man".*

Charity is the ultimate qualifier. Fancy establishing your wacky credentials by sitting in a bath of beans? In the middle of a shopping centre perhaps? Just say you're doing it for Children in Need. No one will bat an eyelid – it's for charity. Would you like to live out your adolescent dreams of being a professional footballer? Take part in a televised football friendly between a bunch of ex-footballers and some celebrities? Simply involve a charitable cause and you will instantly graft some meaning on to this pointless spec-

---

* At least, that's what it sounded like; it could have been "Let Me Entertain You" by Robbie Williams for all I know.

tacle. I mean, it's not as if there's enough real football on the telly already, is it?

Climb a mountain blindfold, walk to the South Pole barefoot, sail around the world backwards and justify the fact that this is no more than something you really want to do by claiming it is a charity awareness-raising exercise.

The wealthy may giveth their time (on an expenses-plus-minimal-fee basis), but it is the poor who giveth the most money. In a speech to the House of Lords in 2004, Lord Joffe highlighted this issue:

> [From 1992 to 2002] personal incomes have risen in real terms on average by more than 25 per cent; personal wealth has more than doubled; the Chancellor of the Exchequer, Gordon Brown, has introduced a range of very attractive tax benefits with the objective of stimulating giving; the charitable sector has become much more professional in fundraising; and the very wealthy have prospered as never before. With all those positives, one would have expected the level of individual giving as a percentage of GDP to have increased dramatically. Instead it has fallen from 1.2 per cent in 1992 to 0.9 per cent in 2002, a fall of 25 per cent.

> [It] emerges that the poor who give to charity give on average three times as much as a proportion of their income as the better off, the top 20 per cent of whom give on average

only 0.7 per cent. So, we find that the poor,
who cannot really afford it, are considerably
more generous than the well-off, who can. This
is even more astonishing when regard is paid to
the statistics that show that the wealthiest 1 per
cent of the population own close to one quarter
of the total marketable wealth, while the
poorest half of the population own between
them only 5 per cent.*

It's not charity's fault; it's ours and those pesky brands
again. US economist Jeremy Rifkin believes that the
modern economy is concept-based. This is epitomised by
Nike, a company that manufactures nothing itself, and is
entirely engaged in selling spurious lifestyle choices. Under
these conditions, Rifkin believes that the economy will
expand to colonise more and more areas of our lives, until
virtually all human experience is mediated by commercial
exchange. As such, charity has become a device for legit-
imising self-gratification and self-promotion.

Similarly, "choice" has lost any real meaning: it has
become simply a buzzword used in mitigation of a corporate action. And be under no illusion, a corporate action
that will have been designed to stick it to the competition
in some way.

Supermarkets don't want you to have any choice. They
want you to buy everything from them: groceries, home
insurance, finance, mobile phones, newspapers, magazines,

---

* Hansard, 26 May 2004, cols 1389, 1390.

DVDs, electrical goods, clothing, home wares, holidays, even kitchen sinks. You might be surprised to know that 10 per cent of UK music downloads are bought at Tesco.com.

The business objective for supermarkets is actually the removal of choice. The average high-street newsagent – WH Smith or Menzies – stocks about 4,500 different magazines each month: the average supermarket stocks around 300. You will probably be able to get a copy of the market-leading film magazine at your local Sainsbury, but you will find it more difficult to buy a copy of one of the others. Joanne Blythman explains:

> Supposedly supermarkets give us this fabulous choice and before supermarkets we were in this state of rationing. It's quite a psychological achievement when you look at how narrow the choice really is. There is a choice, but it's not a qualitative choice. The real variety, the different crops that we used to grow have all gone. Very few people have challenged the supermarket idea that they provide choice.*

Moreover, once you're in there, supermarkets want you to buy *their* products. The supermarkets' promotion of own-label products has shifted competitive forces in favour of retailers.† Not only do own brands make the highest

---

* Joanne Blythman, author of *Shopped*, in an interview with Dan Kieran, *The Idler*, 34.
† Wrigley and Lowe, 2002.

contribution to gross margin, but they drive customer loyalty and enhance the retailers' corporate reputation or brand image. Retailers have developed supply-chain management systems of huge power and complexity, generating huge amounts of data on individual customers from point-of-sale scanners (EPOS data) and loyalty card schemes (over 80 per cent of Tesco sales are made using the club card). They know more about your shopping habits than you do. Clearly this information provides them with a huge competitive advantage in terms of product research. They can easily identify which products are most popular with their customers, and thus which own-label facsimiles are likely to prove the most successful. They are effectively derisking their product development strategy. This gives supermarkets a huge advantage: approximately 85 per cent of new FMCG products (things like packaged food, toiletries and household goods) fail within a year of launch; anything that can mitigate that degree of failure will have a huge effect on the bottom line. Furthermore, retailers' brands now compete head on with manufacturers' brands through shelf placement and packaging, but it's not a level playing field. Unlike those of other suppliers, own-label products do not have to be sold or discounted to supermarket buyers.

Asda and Tesco lead the field in data sharing, which not only gives their suppliers detailed sales information, but can also be used to pressurise them into exclusive agreements.

Supermarkets' move into new markets outside groceries – such as clothing, electrical goods or financial services – is known as "channel blurring". The biggest retailers measure their market share in terms of the retail sector as a whole, rather than just in terms of groceries. Tesco, the UK's biggest retailer, accounts for over 12 per cent of the UK's total retail expenditure. In other words, one in every eight UK retail pounds is spent at Tesco.

And why have we been so ready to sacrifice choice? To gain convenience. The idea of having to wait for something is becoming anathema to us. We want everything now. The consequences of this are visible in the useless things with which we have surrounded ourselves.

I recently visited our local UCGI-Odeon Multi-Centertainment Complex with Niamh, my seven-year-old daughter, to watch the latest instalment of the CGI franchise *Ice Age 2*. If you haven't caught *Ice Age 2* yet, I won't spoil the story for you by telling you there isn't one. It was no more than a series of bite-sized vignettes, beautifully realised in computerised graphic brilliance, of course, but not even loosely held together by narrative. It was like watching an animated *Big Brother* – a group of strangers were thrown together and we watched how they interacted with each other. The film lasted about an hour and a half, but it could easily have lasted fifteen minutes or a lifetime. I expect the franchise will continue in the same manner for quite some time.

As we emerged, jet-lagged from the artificial night of the cinema, into early evening sunshine, we decided, as a special treat, to get something to eat at one of the restaurants on-site. I told Niamh that she could choose the venue for our repast. She weighed up what was on offer – there was plenty of choice: Old Orleans, the American Diner, TGI Friday's, Franky & Benny's, Chiquito, Bitz & Pizza and Burger King. Eventually, overwhelmed by option paralysis, she passed the gauntlet back to me and I exercised my consumer right to choose by having an ersatz American-style grilled meal in one of the above establishments. I can't remember which one it was, but I think it probably doesn't matter.

Maybe there are people out there who prefer TGI Friday's to Old Orleans, and perhaps some of them could even construct a cogent argument for the superiority of Chain A's chicken fajitas over Chain B's. But surely there are few people who could argue that the ability to choose between seven restaurants with near-identical menus, pricing and decor is a defining example of the concept of choice.

And it's not just in the arena of eating in and eating out that taste convergence is happening. Like competition, convenience is the enemy, not the bedfellow, of choice. At risk of appearing obtuse, let me state that it's clear that given the choice between "choice" and "convenience", we choose convenience every time. That means we can kiss any idea of individualism goodbye, because homogenised amenity has become the dominant feature of the most precious commodity we have left: our free time.

## 20 | **Gone In 60 Seconds**

"If work was so good, the rich would have
kept more of it for themselves."
*David Brent, area manager, Wernham Hogg*

The UK has developed a culture of working long hours.
This didn't happen suddenly, but has crept up on us insidi-
ously over the past 30 years. British workers work an average of 43.6 hours per week; in continental Europe the
average is only 40.3. Nearly 4 million people are working
more than 48 hours per week, with one in 25 men working
at least a 60-hour week. All this is going on despite the
European Working Time Directive of 1998, which introduced a 48-hour working week limit.

According to a 2006 report commissioned by the TUC:

> Overwork is forcing workers into unhealthy
> lifestyles as they attempt to reconcile long
> working hours and family responsibilities,
> according to a new report. Half of the parents
> surveyed were unhappy with their work and
> family balance. A majority reported that work
> dominated their lives, and family life suffered
> as a result. Working long hours also led to
> increased levels of stress, resulting in
> irritability, exhaustion and depression.*

---

* TUC, "Time, health and the family: what working families want", *Out of Time*, 2006.

UK workers work the longest hours in Europe. This situation couldn't be any farther away from the technological promises of the 1970s, when, as we have seen, it was believed that we would work six-hour days and four-day weeks, in paperless offices, as robots working tirelessly in a permanent night of windowless factories produced the consumer goods we would need to maximise our surfeit of leisure time.

So much for that, but the impact on our lives of the technological revolution has been as significant as we believed: it's just our understanding of the implications which has proved incorrect (who'd have thought that the future gazers would get something wrong?), and I'd like to look briefly at three areas in which technology has helped to shape a generation of consumers gagging for useless things.

First of all, it is true that technology has fuelled the biggest economic boom in history. We may be working harder, but we're earning proportionally far more than we ever did in the past. Between 1976 and 2006 average earnings rose by almost 650 per cent. Which means that if you're more than six years into your career, you've probably accrued more money than your 1976 counterpart would expect to see in their entire 40-year-plus working career. What's more, you're paying proportionately less tax than they were as well.

Technology has also made it much easier for banks to lend us money. The word "computer" was originally used to describe a human being – usually a woman – who spent all day making tedious mathematical calculations on behalf of banks and financial institutions. Nobody needs to send off to head office for a copy of your financial history any more, they can access it online in a couple of seconds, finding out whether or not you're the kind of assiduous borrower who makes every payment in a timely fashion, or whether you've developed a habit of disappearing regularly off the face of the earth.

Banks like lending us money – it is, after all, how they make theirs – and at the moment they are generously lending us more money than ever before. Consumer borrowing stands at a record high of over £3 trillion. Together with wages, this has created a cash-rich/time-poor society, giving us the means and the incentive to spend more on entertaining ourselves during our precious time away from work. It's a lifestyle that gives us more disposable income than any other generation in history.

There is, of course, a catch. One of the basic laws of economics states that if there is more money in circulation, then people will start charging more for goods: the law of matching supply and demand. Get it wrong and the result is invariably inflation. This was a huge problem for ancient civilisations, particularly the Romans, who didn't understand this fundamental economic law. So in times of hardship they tended to address the situation by minting more denarii (albeit with a lower silver content than normal) and were consistently staggered when this made the situation worse, rather than better.

"But Steve," you reply triumphantly, "surely we're living through a period of low inflation? It's been less than one and a half per cent for pretty much all of the past fifteen years – shows what you know about economics."

But wait! True, official inflation figures have remained low, but they *exclude* house prices. And I'm guessing your house (or houses) constitutes by some way the most expensive purchase you've ever made, or are ever likely to. In 1976, houses generally cost 3.3 times what you earned in a year. The average house price was £12,209 while the average salary was £3,700. In 2006 your house will cost you almost eight times what you earn. The average house price at the time of writing is £188,290, with the average salary at £24,200. For financiers, it's a win-win situation; they lend you more, so you have to borrow more, so they lend you more.

But not all our money goes on our houses. As well as mortgages, HP and personal loans, there are credit cards, debit cards, store cards and loyalty cards. Much of this cash is spent ensuring that we get as much out of diminished leisure time as possible. And here we come to the third and most curious way in which technology has affected our behaviour. Most office workers – and in a service economy, that means most of us – spend most of our time at work sat at a computer. Computers may be synonymous with clinical efficiency, but all the research suggests that the same is not true of people working at them.

The computer's unique capability can be distilled down to the fact that it makes multitasking incredibly simple. The implications of this are far more significant than you might think. In paper-based offices, working in parallel was not an option. Getting all the information and resources together to do Task A made it difficult to do the same for Task B simultaneously and impossible for Task C.

There was no opportunity to edit on the fly, to cut and paste from earlier documents, or fill in the relevant bits of a template. Completing Task A would involve concentration and organisation over a period of time. Editing a book like this one would mean paying somebody to type it up again properly, so ideas had to be organised before they were committed to the page. Today, it can be no more than a few minutes' work to create a discussion document: draw some information from the Web or existing sources, give it a bit of layout and, bang, just like Cillit, you're done!

We can be writing two documents and a presentation simultaneously, while sending an email and bidding for something on eBay. Indeed, as I write this, I'm listening to the new Zero 7 album, making a compilation CD in iTunes and keeping an eye on progress in one of the World Cup quarter-finals. Other than that, you've got my undivided attention.

Computers have taught us to process small pieces of information and enjoy bite-sized narrative, often simultaneously, from multiple sources. But this has been achieved at the expense of being able to concentrate long enough to process complex ideas or narratives. We are entertained on the move by shuffling through songs on our iPods; we no longer sit down to digest entire albums. We prefer the instant hit of the emailed gag to the development of a comic character over three series. We enjoy the ephemeral sugary thrills of spats and intrigue between *Big Brother* contestants or *EastEnders* characters rather than the acquired taste of more intellectually demanding dramas or documentaries.

It was not always the case. Twenty or thirty years ago, high-brow dramas like *Jewel in the Crown* and *Brideshead Revisited* topped the ratings; watched now they seem slow – remarkably slow, in fact – completely lacking in whizz-bang by today's standards, but they are none the worse for that. Current affairs and investigative journalism were still very much a prime-time preserve with *Panorama* and *World in Action* scheduled before most children, let alone their parents, had gone to bed.

At least my generation can remember the olden days; our children have no idea what life was like before computers. Larry Cuban is professor of education at Stanford University; in 2001 he summarised all the existing research on educational computing and drew the following conclusion: "There have been no advances over the past decade that can be confidently attributed to broader access to computers. The link between test-score improvements and computer availability and use is even more contested."

More recently, a University of Munich study of 174,000 students in 31 countries showed that students who frequently use computers performed worse academically than those who used them rarely or not at all.

We avoid depth, balking at anything that might be intellectually challenging or which will force us to think. We really don't want to invest a huge amount of time and effort in getting good at something either. What we want is to be kept mildly entertained. This has provided a huge opportunity for those seeking to make their fortunes by entertaining us. As all areas of human experience are commercialised, our leisure time is becoming more and more formulaic and homogenised. It's a process we actively welcome. The main sociological impact of the World Cup is not the increase in people actively participating in the sport, but the increase in sales of football-themed video games. It's much easier to replicate the skills of Zidane or Ronaldinho vicariously from the comfort of your armchair, through a few judicious thumb and finger moves, sustained by crisps and fizzy drinks, than it is to practise for hour after hour, day after day, month after month, year after year. Simply playing football competitively at any reasonable standard involves achieving a level of fitness that is sadly way beyond the reach of many overweight schoolchildren.

Physical sloth and mental indolence often go hand in hand. Spend too much time online and you could find that your attention span is rapidly reduced. According to Ted Selker, Associate Professor of Media Arts and Science at the Massachusetts Institute of Technology, "Our attention span gets affected by the way we do things. If we spend our time flitting from one thing to another on the web, we can get into a habit of not concentrating."

The Web offers billions of possibilities – the opportunity for instant gratification is always just a click away, a distraction for which we need no encouragement. In their research, Selker's team measured the attention span of the average surfer at about nine seconds.

Surfers are unwilling to dwell on any one website; they are constantly on the lookout for more engaging content and ways to spend their time. Average dwell time per site is a mere 60 seconds. This presents a huge challenge for commercial websites, which rely on their users for revenue and are desperate to keep them there.

Our days have become punctuated by the micro-rush offered by fresh information distractions. Most of us open emails as soon as they arrive, breaking off whatever we're doing to click on the little envelope icon and see what gives (even just writing that sentence made me want to check my inbox). As broadband access becomes ubiquitous, we are prone to taking quick breaks, perhaps to watch a short movie on YouTube, place a bid for an item on eBay or check out the invariably spurious transfer rumours on teamtalk.com.

Much of this activity is pointless. There is no aim to it, no goal, no object: often we don't even know why we're surfing, let alone what we're looking for. We are thrill-seekers in a world of useless information. We have conditioned ourselves to demand quantity over quality. As we have seen, we don't know what we want, but we know we want it now. But more than this, we don't even know why we want it, we just know we want lots of it.

Quantity; the illusion of choice; a quest for the same but slightly different; the familiar with a twist – we are all living slightly different versions of the same vanilla life theme. Our experiences are not vastly different and our aspirations are frighteningly similar.

We live in individually designed but virtually identical magnolia houses; we take the same holidays in geographically different, virtually identical sunshine-filled resorts, where everybody speaks English, the international language of consumption.*

We are invited to vote for opposing political parties peddling virtually identical centre-right politics. We party hard in Vodka Revolution, Wetherspoons and All Bar One, wearing clothes we bought in Gap, Next or Henry Lloyd, having variations on the same conversation about the latest events in *Big Brother, I'm A Celebrity..., Celebrity Love Island, X Factor, Pop Idol* or *Strictly Come Dancing.*

Modern life isn't rubbish, but if it's white-knuckle excitement you're after, you're unlikely to find it here, unless you're prepared to indulge in strong drugs or the ersatz thrills provided by the rollercoaster designers of Alton Towers. Perhaps this explains people's desire to get away from it all: both in actual fact and vicariously.

---

* Again, I apologise if this gives you the impression I live in a teepee, home-educating my kids, weaving my own yogurt and travelling everywhere by bike. I recently took a hugely expensive week's holiday in Gran Canaria. Fiona, my wife, took full credit for booking this budget-busting beano, blaming it on a moment of cerebral weakness, brought about by the birth of our third child, which left her feeling hormonal. The full cost of our six-day break was revealed to me only as we pulled up in a taxi outside our hotel: an intimate affair, housing certainly no more than three thousand people. The surrounding resort had all the authentic charm and character of Mr Blobby, nothing more than a conurbation of shopping centres – it felt as if we never got out of duty-free. On the last day I caved in and bought a Sony PSP for £20 less than it would have cost me over here. I'm ashamed to say it really did make me feel much better. The moral of this story is: I'm only human. Seriously, you wouldn't believe how much money this never-to-be-repeated "experience" cost, which is why I haven't written it down. Email me and I might tell you.

## 21 | **Come With Me and Escape**

"A perpetual holiday is a good working definition of hell."
*George Bernard Shaw, author and playwright*

One of the biggest lies I've ever heard is that "travel broadens the mind". No it bloody well doesn't. Not in my experience or the experience of anybody I've ever met. I've met lots of people who have *claimed* that travel broadened *their* mind, but they were all without exception lying – even if only to themselves.

I'd consider myself reasonably well travelled. I'm no Michael Palin and I've never lived abroad full-time, but I've spent a great deal of time working overseas and of course on holiday. For what it's worth, I know my way round Germany pretty well – I'm as familiar with Hamburg, Nuremberg, Düsseldorf and Munich as I am with most British cities, and I've spent several weeks of my life in Würzburg and Dortmund. The same is true for France and Spain, Italy (to a lesser extent) and, as long as we discount travel too far from any major cities, for Sweden, Norway, Finland, the Netherlands, Turkey, Bulgaria, Portugal and Denmark.

In total I've spent quite a few months in the United States – not just LA, New York and San Francisco either, but the boring bits like Atlanta, Philadelphia and Irvine. I have even appeared on national TV in Argentina (which is a story that might well turn up in another book). And to top all that I've recently spent a bank-breaking week of my life in El Arndale-del-Mar of Gran Canaria.

Thanks in no small part to Sony's wonderful PSP, and aside from the occasional frosty meetings with my company's German distributor – "It is answers I am wanting, Herr McKevitt, not more of your English bullshit," that sort of thing – I can honestly say I've enjoyed virtually every minute of it. What I can't honestly say is it made me a better person.

Let us then set the concept of a year out against this landscape. I was eighteen and studying at university before I became aware that such a year out existed. This was 1985 and university education was not the matter of course it is today. I was the first member of my family ever to attend university. This was at a time when "university" meant an elite Ivy League of institutions that only 6 per cent of the population were privileged enough to attend, not the local college of higher education. They even paid you to go, for Chrissakes.

I met one of my best mates at university, a guy called Jules. Jules is a year older than me, and it transpired that he had taken a year out to pick oranges on a farm in Israel. The farm was called a kibbutz, which afforded it a little bit of glamour, I suppose, and the weather was always sunny, but apart from a return flight, was this really any better than how I'd spent my own summer: making cardboard boxes in a factory at 1p each. Making cardboard boxes is exceedingly boring, but the exercise was made far more exciting, if decidedly less enterprising, by the willingness of the smiling girl on the machine next to mine to rendezvous in the storeroom on a daily basis. I almost looked forward to going into work.

The point is, few who were at university with me some twenty years ago would remember the fact that I spent a summer making cardboard boxes, but I'll bet a small fortune if you said the phrase "When I was in Israel, right ..." everyone who had encountered him back then would immediately recognise that you were having a dig at Jules.* His time spent travelling has undoubtedly made an impression on him, and he was determined it would make an impression on us.

Today it is much more common for graduates to take a gap year before starting work. I don't know the figures for how many students take this option, but based on the CVs we receive whenever we're looking to recruit a graduate, I'd say it was pretty much all of them.

The fact is that travel is no substitute for a personality. Dullards who go travelling return dullards, only now they are armed with dull stories about unfamiliar places. I suppose we can just be thankful that so few of them play golf. The Third World is treated like some kind of theme park in which white middle-class kids can undergo some kind of epiphany. Yet their experiences, the occasional murder by poverty-stricken locals notwithstanding, are remarkably similar. Bungee jumping in Australia, kayaking across New Zealand's South Island, swimming with whales off Tierra del Fuego, swinging with orang-utans in Borneo, trekking across the Inca trail to Machu Picchu. Why can't we be honest and call these things what they are: holidays undertaken by tourists?

A gap year is nothing more than a long vacation, pro-

---

* Don't feel sorry for him. Jules is now at the *News of the World*, so people digging up the past is second nature to him.

crastination in the face of a lifetime of toil, delivering an experience that is as different from the next person's as a break in Majorca is from one in Kos. Not a bad thing per se – indeed, for the person undertaking the gap year it's a very good thing – but don't kid yourself that your path to personal enlightenment is going to make the world a better place. People don't have to see poverty in the Third World to realise that it's going to take more than wearing one of those armbands and buying a Coldplay album to make it history. But who wouldn't need a twelve-month holiday after spending three long years studying for up to eight hours each week, for almost thirty weeks a year?

Again, this is not meant to sound like sour grapes. I don't begrudge the bright young things their (extended) moment in the sun, but I don't see any direct tangible benefits from the increased numbers of those who have had their minds broadened by travel. We don't appear to be more ethical in our foreign policy, and we aren't curbing our levels of consumption as a result. There's more head-shaking and hand-wringing at the desperate plight of those in the Third World, but beyond the rise of faux-anti-Establishment but ultimately mainstream capitalist brands like Innocent, Pret A Manger and Ben and Jerry's, and attendance at awareness-raising free concerts, I can see precious little in the way of lifestyle-changing mass action

On a more personal, selfish level I just don't want to be subjected to an aural slide show of each amazing event; to be fascinated when they tell me they went on a train in Bolivia; to be awestruck that they picked grapes in Chile; to marvel at the beads bought off a migrant worker in

Bangalore; or to listen to the music that I'm certain must have sounded brilliant in context, during the heat of the local festival at which they first heard it, but now sounds just so shit in the office on a miserable December afternoon. In these circumstances it's always tempting to point at their Nike trainers and ask whether they were bought direct from the kid in Vietnam who actually made them.

The patronising myth that the Third World offers enlightenment on the way to overcoming the problems of modern life is as distasteful as the consumption that drives the poverty gap and not a million miles away from the jingoistic concept of "the noble savage". Poor people in the Third World don't want us to live like them: they want to live like us. Which explains why, when you turn up with the equivalent of several years' salary in your rucksack, you might find there are a few people who want to take that off you. At least the year-outers have the excuse of youth on their side.

The BBC's *Get a New Life* is just one of many TV programmes that exploit our dissatisfaction with modern life. Its central conceit is that the presenters, the gruff and pragmatic Scott Huggins and the authoritative but foxy Melissa Porter, help families to realise their dreams of a life less ordinary in foreign climes. The families in question have just two weeks to pack up their troubles and prepare for a new life abroad. Melissa and Scott are on hand to help them search for jobs and a new home, but only for the first month; after that the family has to make a choice: will they make a go of it, or return home with their dreams in tatters, applying themselves to their former job at the cardboard box factory with new-found enthusiasm?

That at least is the show's tantalising set-up. In fact much of the entertainment factor is provided by the jaw-dropping lack of awareness typically exhibited by participating families. Generally, they seem amazed to find that living abroad is like being in a foreign country. Who would have guessed that forms would be printed in the local language, that nobody speaks English or that there is less of a market for their Web design business in Mombasa than there was in Manchester? At the end of the month they realise that spending fourteen hours a day cleaning swimming pools, in 100-degree heat, followed by friendless evenings drinking bottled water together on the veranda, pondering how Stockport County are getting on, is simply a warmer form of drudgery. By the end of the month they are usually biting Melissa and Scott's arms off for the tickets home. Most of the time we leave them where we found them, as they make the face-saving claim that they'll definitely go back one day now they know what's involved, even though they'll never get more help to find a job, a house and a life than they've just had.

One memorable episode involved a middle-class couple from Bristol approaching retirement age. Their time was spent playing the organ in church, going for walks and tending the garden of their 1930s semi, but they had spent many happy holidays in Mozambique, and thought, you know, what the heck, let's go and live there. Even the usually gung-ho Scott and Melissa uttered an uncharacteristic note of caution: weren't they worried about, well, the phenomenally high crime rate, corruption and unstable government? The couple turned to each other and laughed –

they'd been expecting this – no, of course they weren't, most Mozambicans they'd met were very friendly people and they felt much safer in Maputo than they did in some parts of Bristol. Scott and Melissa shrugged, waved their magic wands and made their dreams come true.

It's even worse than you think. True, most Mozambicans are friendly, law-abiding people, but a few of them aren't. Our couple found themselves a lovely apartment in Maputo with a sea view and on their first day bought some lovely fresh vegetables from the friendly market traders outside.

After just a couple of days, however, it became apparent that the friendly square outside changed character once the sun had set – gone were the friendly market traders, replaced by pimps, drug addicts and prostitutes. Our couple were mugged on the way back from church and quickly became prisoners in their own home: once literally when they were held at knife point while their flat was systematically emptied. News of their arrival had clearly travelled fast. And if that wasn't enough, even God himself got in on the act. A minor tsunami finally put paid to any idea of making a go of it, by flooding their second-floor flat and leaving the floors covered in a two-inch layer of sand and raw sewage. At least it explained the lack of carpets. Needless to say, they were on their way home quicker than you could say "one way please", but still had the good grace to leave us with the claim that they would definitely be back. One day. Perhaps.*

Still, if the real world offers little in the way of escape,

* Yeah, right!

there is another way out of this life: a gateway to worlds of excitement, adventure and untold riches that you won't even need to leave the house for. And all for just 19 dollars a month.

Like many small boys, ten-year-old me tended to get obsessed by things quite easily. Allegedly this has something to do with the gene for autism. Some medical experts think that all males are autistic; it is just a question of the degree. Some of us never grow out of our childhood passions. Many adults have model train sets, or extensive collections of beer mats, stamps or cigarette cards; others are experts in some aspect of exceedingly parochial local history (say, bus timetables). Then there are football numpties, trainspotters, twitchers (or birdwatchers) and ridge-walkers – the list goes on. Call them hobbies if it makes you feel better.

Well, I'm glad to say I grew out of this one. It was towards the end of my cub scout years that I began exploring the obsessive side of my personality in earnest. By way of limbering up I'd experimented with the hobbyist equivalent of soft drugs: some recreational football card collecting led to collating as much information as possible about the Poland national football team.* Sharks (after seeing *Jaws*) were next, the subject of numerous paintings and at least one class show-and-tell,† followed by jet packs (obvi-

---

* Bizarrely, I supported them in the 1974 and 1978 World Cups with so much passion I almost didn't notice England weren't there. Deyna, Lato and Szarmach were my heroes.

† I showed the class a book called *The Shark Attack Files*, now sadly out of print, which contained nothing more than accounts of shark attacks, taken

ously) and *Doctor Who*. But all this was pretty much decriminalised Class C dabbling, compared to the free-basing, all-encompassing Class A pathological obsession I was about to have with Advanced Dungeons and Dragons.

Steve Hill, the country's funniest video games reviewer, once pondered whether there were any more shameful words in the English language than "Dungeons and Dragons". I know what he means. When I flick through my old football cards, or think of Poland's red Adidas away kit, or even catch sight of one of the ubiquitous shark documentaries on the Discovery Channel, I still feel a small frisson of excitement, a reminder perhaps of innocent childhood memories and happy times. Not so my memories of Advanced Dungeons and Dragons. Like many other reformed addicts, the idea of playing AD&D, as we called it, now makes my skin crawl, but between the ages of eleven and fourteen I really didn't think it was humanly possible to have more fun.

Why? Well, first of all, those were more enlightened times. Today it's okay to be into *Lord of the Rings* – it's the biggest-grossing film franchise ever; grown men talk openly about orcs, trolls and walking trees. Believe me, 30 years ago the cool kids didn't read J. R. R. Tolkien. In fact, if you did, it automatically meant that you weren't cool: as if by magic, you'd lose any ability you may have had for sport, your trousers would flare slightly, your hair would

---

from what I can only presume was some kind of file. It had a fantastic strapline: "Jaws was all fiction, this is all fact!" As I recall, it certainly lived up to its gory promise. And of course, I learned nothing about sharks at all.

grow over your ears and you'd find yourself squinting at things you could previously see quite well. And don't confuse this version of the game with the Dungeons and Dragons that was heavily marketed from the mid-1980s onwards, aimed at kids and supported by a very popular cartoon series tie-in: I'm talking about the hardcore 1970s original.

Originally published in 1974 by TSR, Dungeons and Dragons was a set of rules for fantasy role-playing. If that last sentence hasn't got you slavering in anticipation, then I'd say it will be almost impossible for you to ever understand the appeal of AD&D, but I'll do my best. AD&D was a fantasy role-playing game in which players acted the part of a character – a hobbit, a wizard or a knight, for example – in a story that had been prepared in advance by a referee called a Dungeon Master (or DM for short – we were big on acronyms and abbreviations). Games were played each weekend with a bunch of friends – "The Party" – going on an adventure under the aegis of the nominated DM. The party might, for example, undertake a quest involving wandering round an imaginary dungeon in search of a princess/magical artefact/holy relic that needed to be returned to its original owner. The party would spend most of its time fighting imaginary monsters, finding imaginary treasure and solving occasional puzzles. Every time something happened, dice would be rolled to determine the outcome.

Beyond that, let's just say it is one of those things you either get or you don't. And it might sound like a quaint parlour game, but to us AD&D was a credo, and as such could be played only one way: with poker-faced seriousness. Sure, on paper AD&D was a formulaic game of make-believe. You could play it using pens, paper, funny multi-sided dice (and, if you were really keen, small lead figures you spent days painting), and yes, you would hang out with elves and fairies and fight dragons and ogres, but don't think this was kids' stuff. We treated its rules with a gravitas usually afforded only to articles of faith and spent hours discussing the best combinations of weapons, spells and character class.

I was normally the DM and consequently spent almost every waking hour, if not actually drawing maps on graph paper and filling exercise books with detailed narrative descriptions of each room and what was in it, then at least thinking about doing it. The rule books themselves were like telephone directories filled with stats, tables, descriptions of monsters, treasure, magic spells and unbelievably bad artwork. As if playing the thing wasn't geeky enough, the game even had its own smug vocabulary, which couldn't have been better designed to highlight your inadequateness to anyone overhearing. You would talk of an interesting *scenario* you'd created in a Tolkienesque *milieu*; of battles measured in *mêlée rounds*, of *armour class, HTK* (hits to kill), *saving throws, character classes, modules, demi-humans, triple elves, fighter-thieves* and *NPCs* (non-player characters).

Play would take place weekly on Saturday afternoons. The whole gang would assemble to take part in an exciting quest. In between we'd meet in smaller groups for which we'd have to create non-player characters. These sessions were usually played out against a soundtrack of progressive rock music: Yes and early Genesis or Hawkwind were best, but Van Der Graaf Generator, Jethro Tull and Camel were also acceptable. Suffice to say, we didn't have a girlfriend between us.

To give you an idea of what it was like, here is the story of a typical Saturday afternoon's play from around 1980. This week we're playing at David Carney's house.

There are six of us: Shaun, Tommy, the lachrymose Tim, the slightly older and more streetwise Tony, David and me. I'm DMing and, if I do say so myself, I have cooked up something pretty special for the guys. I've been bedridden for a week with a virus, but my indisposition has not been wasted. I have been busy with coloured pens, rulers, graph paper and exercise books creating, in reasonable detail, the city of Man-Mantioch. Playing the role of their characters – Tommy and Shaun play armour-clad fighters, Tim an elvish wizard, Tony a dwarven warrior, while Dave is playing his favourite character, Ranulf the Halfling, who's a kind of hobbit-thief thing – the party will take part in an adventure that will rely on their brains as much as brawn for success. More *Morse* and *Marple* than *Conan the Barbarian*, I feel.

Hand-painted lead figures representing each of the characters are placed on the reverse of a Subbuteo pitch in the middle of the table and, dice at the ready, our adventure gets under way.

The sun is setting as our party arrives, after a long journey across the Whispering Desert, at the gatehouse of Man-Mantioch. They make it just in time before the city gate closes at sundown, and their first task is to find a place to stay for the night. They are directed to a number of taverns, but they all seem to be full because of a religious festival that is taking place at the Temple of Xiobarg (told you it was reasonably detailed). Getting nowhere, they are told about an inn called the Green Manticore, which allegedly has rooms to spare. Making their way to a rather insalubrious part of town (they've no idea I'm subtly guiding them there), they find the run-down hostelry and book two rooms for the night. They pick up a few bits of useful information from the other punters in the bar, take a decision to rob one of the local temples the next day and retire for the night.

At about four in the morning, Goldfin the dwarf (played by Tony) awakes to find that two shadowy figures have bound and gagged his room-mate Ranulf the Halfling, with a view to kidnapping him (the dolts had forgotten to leave someone on guard!). Goldfin bravely gives chase, but his little legs are not swift enough and Ranulf is lost. Returning to his room, Goldfin finds that in the struggle Ranulf managed to tear a scarf off one of his assailants. The scarf is weighted at one end and further inspection reveals a secret pocket in which is a note wrapped around a medallion. Goldfin wakes the others, and on further inspection the party finds that the medallion contains an engraving of a flaming dagger. The note says:

> Meet me under the crescent moon at sunset,
> Yours in honour and death,
> Mordigan.

Now this is where the adventure starts. I've laid out a series of puzzles, clues and riddles for the party to solve which will lead to the rescue of Ranulf. There will be treachery and trickery, twists and turns, danger and death – all the ingredients of a great adventure in fact.

The first clue is easy to solve. All the party has to do is ask anyone whether they know what the crescent moon is and they will discover that it's a famous landmark in the town. Here they can intercept Mordigan and find out more about the Flaming Dagger (which is in fact a secret cult that is planning a human/halfling sacrifice in three days' time. They will be given further clues to help them find Ranulf and met Ashana, a beautiful female warrior who is also looking for the Flaming Dagger to help her find her long-lost father – yes, that's right, she's really a baddie!).

Of course, this is what would have happened if Ian McKellen had been playing the wizard, or if Orlando Bloom was one of the fighters, but unfortunately all these characters were played by twelve-year-old boys.

Things had already become a bit fractious when Ranulf the Halfling complained that I was picking on him.

"Why are they fucking kidnapping me?"

"Because you're the weakest."

"No I'm not, the wizard is. Look: I've got eleven strength, he's only got nine."

"Well, because you're a halfling."

"Now you're making it up as you go along!"

"Look, the DM's word is final, it says so in the *Dungeon Master's Guide*."

"Well, this is my house and I say 'Bollocks to the rules!'"

Once he'd calmed down we continued. A brief period of chastisement followed Goldfin's failed rescue attempt and there was another argument about why he didn't call for help. During his abduction, Dave had told Tony to call for help. As DM I ruled that as Ranulf was gagged he couldn't have asked Goldfin to do this, so Tony couldn't take that option. The DM's word is final, and obviously, I needed one of them to be kidnapped for the story to work.

With Ranulf gone, we ruled that Dave could no longer communicate with the others verbally. He could communicate with the DM by passing notes. Several of these were very abusive.

Now all the party had to do was effect a rescue. Unfortunately, possibly as a consequence of the argument, possibly because they were stupid, they seemed to have forgotten that it was a flaming dagger engraved on the coin, and were interrogating the innkeeper to find out what he knew about the "Fiery Hand". In fact interrogate is too tame a word: Mossad, the KGB and the Chilean military police could all learn a thing or two about interrogation from twelve-year-old boys. Unsurprisingly the innkeeper knew nothing about the "Fiery Hand", so they killed him and burned his pub to to ground.

Rather than follow my carefully laid path of Mcguffins, they decided their "strategy" would be to conduct a series of house-to-house enquiries. They would ask residents whether they knew what the Fiery Hand was or where Ranulf was being kept, and if they answered in the negative, they'd kill them and set fire to their house. Even the Stasi would have found their approach a little harsh. What followed was nothing more than three hours of rolling dice. There was no story – as such – and at the end my beautiful city had been razed to the ground. There was one other minor point. In the process, they managed to burn down the building in which Ranulf was being held hostage. It was not so much his death which precipitated the end of the game, more Dave's acrimonious reaction, which involved ripping his character sheet into a thousand pieces, throwing them at Tommy (who was holding the torch) and systematically smashing his room up.

Despite all this, it's not the activity itself I find so difficult to stomach – ignominious though it was – but rather just how seriously everybody took it. For a start, we routinely hated other groups of kids in the school who played it, because they didn't play it properly. We were like the AD&D Taliban, we'd spend far less time playing the game than we did laughing at the way everyone else we knew played it. We'd mock the ridiculous lack of realism involved in *their* version of the game. We poured scorn on the fact that *they* didn't understand the rules for encumbrance, and did impressions of how *their* overloaded characters must have fought. We'd openly scoff at the ludicrous system *they* had in place for the distribution of experience points.

I remember one of the gang writing a parody of one of *their* games and pinning it to the school noticeboard, which caused much mirth and amusement among my fellow AD&Ders. The text focused on a minor misunderstanding someone had about the rule for establishing who had the initiative in a round of combat. I don't think John Cleese could possibly have got a better response when he unveiled the Dead Parrot Sketch to his fellow Pythons (a sketch, needless to say, we all knew by heart).

It was music which saved us in the end. Fortunately, I didn't have enough money to fund both hobbies, and more importantly I realised I'd probably never meet a girl who was into Dungeons and Dragons. I wasn't the first to go. Shortly after David smashed his own room up in memory of Ranulf the Halfling, my best mate Shaun announced he wouldn't be turning up to paint figures at my house that evening because he was taping John Peel. Soon arguments over the nuances of armour class and whether female dwarves had beards were replaced with equally pointless but equally heated debates about which Rip Rig and Panic album* was best and whether or not the Teardrop Explodes had sold out by appearing on *Top of the Pops*. The rule books, lead figures and prog albums went up into the loft to be replaced by *Melody Maker*, John Peel and Cabaret Voltaire. The people were the same, the anal conversations were the same, the level of obsession was the same – the only thing that changed was the subject matter and the fact that this is one obsession I've never grown out of.

For obsessive adolescents growing up in the early 1980s, there was really only music. Football was played on Saturdays and TV coverage was restricted to two high-lights packages (of two games each) shown on Saturday and Sunday afternoons. The were no digital TV channels, no computer games, no World Wide Web, no men's fash-

---

* If you're interested, it's definitely the 1982 album *I Am Cold*. The vocals of Neneh Cherry render it far more accessible than its 1981 predecessor *God*, which, in this instance, is a good thing.

ion, no mobile phones (and therefore no txtng). My interest in music was supported by an information network that was by today's standards somewhat limited, to say the least. AD&D was okay if you'd never wondered what it might be like to kiss a girl, as perhaps was trainspotting. Even recreational drugs seemed far less freely available than they are today. I was at university before I'd even seen somebody smoking cannabis, let alone experimented with it myself. Which, obviously, I never, ever have.

I stopped playing AD&D in February 1981. I sold my rule books and associated paraphernalia for a not inconsiderable amount of money, and it's fair to say never really spoke about it again (until now). Had I been asked to use that money to make a bet, I'd have comfortably predicted that fantasy role-playing would remain the preserve of the few, about as likely to trouble the mainstream as Rip Rig and Panic.

But as we've learned, predicting the future is a difficult thing to get right. In 1921, Thomas Edison predicted that the motion picture would replace the textbook by 1927, and similarly my prediction that fantasy role-playing would fail to cross over makes me look a bit of a tit.

The dice and rule books have gone, but today fantasy role-playing is big business. As you may know, in scientific terms I have the greatest respect for organs like *New Scientist* and *The Lancet* and even the Nobel Academy, but for me the benchmark for scientific thinking is BBC2's *Horizon*. *Horizon* spends so much time offering different scenarios for the end of the world it's a wonder you're actually around to read this and haven't been killed by:

global warming, global dimming, the new ice age, freak waves, super-volcanoes, super-massive black holes, comets and asteroids, solar flares, or the melting ice caps.

In one rare edition, which dealt only with the end of civilisation rather than the entire world, viewers were asked to consider, like Descartes, that what we understand as the world about us might in fact be nothing more than a simulation. Imagine that computers and computer graphics have become so powerful that they can make exact three-dimensional copies of the world about us populated with beings who think and feel just as we do.*

Oxford University's Dr Nick Bostrum explains:

> There would be a lot more simulated people like you than there would be original non-simulated ones. And then you've got to think, hang on, if almost everybody like me are simulated people and just a tiny minority are non-simulated ones then I am probably one of the simulated ones rather than one of the exceptional non-simulated ones. In other words you are almost certainly living in an ancestor simulation right now.

What he's saying is that this might all be just one big computer game. It isn't – or if it is, it's the only one I've ever played without any crash bugs or glitches – but the point he's making is really quite interesting. Imagine if you could

* "Time Trip", *Horizon*, BBC2, 18 December 2003.

live in a virtual world that was "better" (defined by your own criteria) than this one, but seemed just as real. And that you could live there with all your family and friends. Well, we're not quite there yet, but millions of people around the world are almost doing just that.

Massive, Multi-player, Online Games (or MMOGs) are huge virtual worlds created and populated in exactly the way that Bostrum describes. There are many of these games, and their setting is typically either futuristic sci-fi and space guns or a *Lord of the Rings*/Advanced Dungeons and Dragons fantasy world. Anyone can play. You pay a subscription each month, create an in-game character, or avatar, for yourself – it can even look like you if you want – and then you're free to explore and do pretty much what you want.

If you play one of the more established games like Everquest or World of Warcraft, you'll find there are millions of other people "living" there as well as many more simulated – or non-player – characters, and monsters. The games worlds are huge: even the smallest cover hundreds of square miles, with cities, castles, forests, oceans and even their own economy. Some people have been playing for years and, as you would imagine, have amassed a significant amount of wealth and power. I was once visiting a friend who edits a video games magazine when one of his staff asked to be allowed to go home early so he could water his hydroponics station (he was playing Star Wars Generations). I also had somebody turn down an all-expenses paid trip to LA because he needed the time to devote to Ultima Online. Apparently he had discovered some black dye in the woods outside the city and planned to sell it at the market on Saturday with a Welsh guy he'd met on a virtual fishing trip. In so many ways, after hearing all that, I was very glad he'd declined.

In an attempt to broaden the appeal of MMOGs beyond orcs, goblins and hydroponics, game designers – and undoubtedly more than a few marketing people – have started looking elsewhere for inspiration, somewhere closer to home. The patronising title says it all: Second Life is an MMOG set in a virtual city just like the ones in this world. The game does exactly what it says: gives its estimated 300,000 human residents the opportunity to have a different life in the virtual world to the one they "enjoy" in the real world. Inevitably, this involves having more sex. It's not so much a better world as a more tawdry one. Swinging appears to be compulsory; your real-world appearance will be no bar to virtual promiscuity. You can even spice things up by buying some virtual sex toys from a virtual sex shop and then watch your avatar take part in an orgy. Second Life residents enthuse pneumatically about their sex lives on message boards and blogs: "Already on my short travels there, I've had many kinds of sex that I wouldn't even think of doing in real life." One can only presume: like the kind that involves another person.

Games like World of Warcraft or Everquest are taken so seriously that the in-game currency has an actual value and the virtual world a GDP bigger than that of some African states. Starting the game as a novice can be daunting and tedious. You'll be a lowly peasant with no money, weapons or power, which you'll quickly find is as dull in

Everquest as it is in the real world. You've got two choices: undertake a series of drudge jobs tarted up as quests – like clearing the village of rats or spending hours chopping firewood and selling it for a few copper pieces – and get used to the fact that fighting dragons and owning your own castle is still a distant dream, or buy a ready-made character on eBay. The latter is not a soft option, because it takes so long to build them up that decent characters can be quite expensive. Today, for example, I found a Level 70 Half-Elf Rogue (dunno what that is) and a Level 70 Warrior available for just $2,000 the pair. How long, I wonder, before, you can buy super-deluxe golden strap-on dildos, for exclusive use in Second Life?

Selling built-up characters, magic weapons or gold pieces online is big business. Especially in South-East Asia, where a single MMOG can have hundreds of thousands of human players at any one time. This opportunity is being exploited by some scurrilous entrepreneurs called Adina Farmers.

Adina is the name of the in-game currency, and what the farmers have done is to set up a few computers and hire kids to not so much play the game as stand next to a monster and fight it until it dies and drops some treasure, wait for it to re-spawn and repeat. For ever.

The resulting booty is sold online. The companies behind the game take quite a dim view of this sort of thing, but are powerless to do anything about it. While it is completely legal, it does rather go against the spirit of the game. But this enterprise has in turn given rise to a bizarre online phenomenon.

Clearly many of the 80,000 human players are not happy with the Adina Farmers coming in and ruining their game, and feel that something had to be done about it. For some reason, playing the role of a female dwarf confers a slight advantage in the game, and as such it has become the character of choice for Adina Farmers. This makes them relatively easy to spot. Taking the law into their own hands, the human players have banded together into what can only be described as lynch mobs, with the specific aim of hunting down and killing every female dwarf they come across. The results are quite unnerving: it's like watching a virtual reconstruction of a Ku Klux Klan rally, only with elves and real wizards.

It's easy to mercilessly stereotype the people who play these games – which is no reason not to; many in-game maidens fair are no doubt sexually confused teenage boys from Switzerland who have eaten too many doughnuts – but the people deserving our pity are surely those who buy characters and magic items. For them, even trying to escape the real world is too much effort. Why bother going through the inconvenience of working for something and reaping the rewards of toil when you can simply buy yourself success, like a CGI Roman Abramovich?

For me this just goes to show what we humans are best at: ruining stuff. Things went wrong the moment someone thought, "Fantastic firework display! Hmm, I wonder what would happen if I pointed this rocket at him?"

No matter what it is – atomic energy, computers, television, cameras, internal combustion engines, medical advances, even the Good News of Jesus – whenever someone comes up with a good idea, our default response is to immediately try to think of a negative use for it: nuclear warheads, identity theft, reality TV, tanks, transplant organ theft, the Spanish Inquisition. A thing of beauty is not a joy for ever; it's just a challenge.

"Work, Buy, Consume, Die"
*The Designers Republic*

Ten-year-old me wanted to live in a future of jet packs, Raquel Welch clones and holidays on Mars, but as Oscar Wilde said, "There's only one thing worse than not getting what you want, and that's getting what you want." I don't know when he said this – I assume it was before he went to Pentonville and found out that not getting what you want can be really shit sometimes – but I do know what he means.

Thirty years on, I'm cynical enough to realise that jet packs wouldn't have made my life any better – there would have been rules and regulations, unfortunate mid-air collisions, jet-pack larcenists, air rage, jet-pack traffic cops, speed limits and air-speed cameras. Likewise holidaying on Mars would be all well and good until easyJet opened up a route to its satellite Phobos, making it accessible to hoi polloi and turning it into a popular stag party location.

The world is full of useless things because of, not despite, us. Our relentless pursuit of convenience has made us wealthier and our lives faster, but it hasn't made us happier.

In July 2006 a survey of the 178 nations on Planet Earth ranked the UK a rather lowly 108th. The index was based on consumption levels, life expectancy and happiness rather than the usual indicators such as GDP.

One of the authors of the report, Nic Marks, explained,

"It is clear that no single nation listed in the index has got everything right, but it does reveal patterns that show how we might better achieve long and happy lives."

Topping the poll was the small Pacific island state of Vanuatu. With a population of just 209,000, the island has an economy that is built around little more than agriculture and tourism. The rest of the top ten was surprisingly dominated by Latin American countries, like Colombia, more famous in the UK media for cocaine trafficking and shooting their under-achieving World Cup footballers. It would seem we have much to learn from the Colombians. Among the world's largest economies, Germany is ranked 81st, with the USA coming in a moribund 150th.

The report found that while living standards have improved dramatically over the past 50 years, we're no happier than we were during the years of post-war austerity. The main source of happiness remains human relationships, which have been sacrificed to some extent in preference to economic growth.

We are not just more miserable either, we're angrier. The UK has the highest incidence of road rage in the world, bar South Africa (which, given the number of drive-by shootings there, is some way out in front). One in three of us are not on speaking terms with our neighbours, and 5 per cent have had a fight with the person living next door; 27 per cent of nurses have been attacked at work and 66 per cent of all absences from work are stress related.

Our money isn't making us happy: we can buy a new BMW for less than £200 per month, which means we no longer have to walk anywhere; we take three foreign holidays a year and still have enough left for plasma-screen TVs, iPods and ready meals. We need to be shown things to spend our money on but we don't need them and they don't make us happy. For many people it's not enough to have one house – they want two.

Michael Palin, the former Python who found a second career as a postmodern Alan Whicker, has lived in the same house since 1968. He bought it once he started getting a steady income from the BBC and, despite amassing considerable fame and fortune, he never moved. He was happy where he was and saw that friends who had second homes were constantly fretting about plumbers and repairs. "I now realise that you can waste an awful lot of time buying things, and I never had that time.'*Time is one thing we all claim we want more of; the irony is that while we believe that convenience buys us more time, it has given us nothing of the sort. We can get everything now if we want it. It's just that not everything is worth having.

---

* *The Idler*, 37, May 2006.

# Appendix 1:
# Why the World Is Full of Useless Things in 300 words

*by Steve McKevitt*

For those of us growing up in the 1970s, science was a panacea. We all looked forward to a future of leisure and amenity forged in the white heat of the technological revolution: windowless factories staffed by robots, paperless offices, four-day weeks – nothing less than the end of want.

The future we've ended up with is very different. Our amazing capacity for overconfidence coupled with an endemic lack of self-awareness has led to a cash-rich, time-poor society where the greatest effort is put not into improving lives, but into making them worse.

We have become ignorant of the world around us. We have no idea how 99 per cent of the stuff we use works and are prepared to believe absolutely everything we read, see and hear in the mass media, forming black-and-white opinions based on only a tiny amount of information.

We are happy to accept second best so long as we are kept mildly entertained, fed and watered. We equate material wealth with success and nothing makes us happier than seeing someone less capable than ourselves; if they're really good at being useless, we'll turn them into major celebrities.

We've put a price tag on every area of our lives – even charity – and convince ourselves that because we've got convenience, we've got choice. Even when we try to get away from it all, we can't help cutting corners.

The world is full of useless things because we've made it that way. It's not a bad world, but if only we demonstrated the tiniest amount of collective ambition it could be a whole lot better. The first step is to demand more from ourselves and refuse to settle for facsimile lifestyles that are available in magnolia, beige or vanilla.

# Appendix 2:
# Why the World Is Full of Useless Things in 300 words

*By Microsoft Word Auto-Summarizer*


If you're not abusive, he might even reply, "A kids' product? It's my first time."

Home Creative Studio – most people will tell you TV studios are surprisingly small.

Read on, if you dare. For a start, the concept of daytime TV didn't exist. Mum laughed as well. In short this was a time of big scientific leaps forward and people expected these big scientific leaps to continue.

Many people were affected by them.

"So if he was on *Mastermind*, he'd get every single question right?" Ironically, the world is now dominated by people who think that they are.

If you didn't get it, don't worry – most people have no idea how any of the basic utilities work. Not even the people selling them.

I get calls at home and at work from people asking me whether I'm happy with my electricity supply, whether I'd like to see if they can supply it cheaper.

Low earnings are much more likely if one has poor basic skills than if one has good basic skills. A bit like Biros or Hoovers, all bottled water at this time was called Perrier water. A Boeing 727?

If I'm not mistaken, there are 60 million people in the UK. What if there were more channels?

Even today, bored people become restless people. Reality TV is serving television well. If reality TV is the Ritalin of the people then celebrity is the crack cocaine.

After all, if Jade's got it then why can't we? If [India] took to similar economic exploitation, it would strip the world bare like locusts. Our free time. Thrill-seekers in a world of useless information.

I've never lived abroad full-time, but I've spent a lot of time there on holiday and a great deal of time working overseas.

Call them hobbies if it makes you feel better.